THE AIVF GUIDE TO FILM & VIDEO DISTRIBUTORS

BY KATHRYN BOWSER

FIVF

FOUNDATION
FOR INDEPENDENT
VIDEO AND FILM

A publication of the Foundation for Independent Video and Film, Inc.

Ruby Lerner
Executive Director

Pamela Calvert
Project Coordinator

Daniel Christmas
Design

The Foundation for Independent Video and Film (FIVF) is supported in part through the generous contributions of the Center for Arts Criticism, Con Edison, The John D. and Catherine T. MacArthur Foundation, National Endowment for the Arts, National Video Resources, New York City Department of Cultural Affairs, The New York Community Trust, New York State Council on the Arts, the Rockefeller Foundation, The Andy Warhol Foundation for the Visual Arts, Inc., and the members of the Association of Independent Video and Filmmakers.

Special thanks to the Florian Loan Fund of the Funding Exchange and the National Endowment for the Arts Challenge Grant Program.

As the media distribution field changes rapidly, we urge you to contact distributors directly before sending tapes and promotional materials, to ensure that the information listed herein is accurate and up-to-date.

The Foundation for Independent Video and Film, Inc. (FIVF), is a nonprofit, tax-exempt educational foundation dedicated to the promotion of video and film. FIVF publishes *The Independent*, the leading monthly magazine on issues of concern to the field. It is affiliated with the Association of Independent Video and Filmmakers (AIVF), the largest association of independent media makers in the country. AIVF provides a range of programs and services to the field including access to health and production insurance; trade and publication discounts; informational and educational programs and seminars; and national legislative advocacy.

For AIVF membership information:
Association of Independent Video and Filmmakers
304 Hudson Street, 6th Floor
New York, NY 10013
(212) 807-1400 tel
(212) 463-8519 fax
aivffivf@aol.com
http://www.virtualfilm.com/AIVF

AIVF/FIVF staff: Ruby Lerner, executive director; Pamela Calvert, director of programs and services; Ellen Barker, resource/development director; Leslie Singer, director of administration; Patricia Thomson, editor, *The Independent*; Laura D. Davis, advertising director, *The Independent*; Johnny McNair, information services coordinator; Leslie Fields, membership coordinator; Judah Friedlander, membership associate; Cleo Cacoulidis, advocacy associate; Lisa Smith, resource/development assistant; Adam Knee, editorial assistant, *The Independent*.

ISBN 0-9622448-3-X

Table of Contents

It is with great pride that the Foundation for Independent Video and Film (FIVF) and the Association of Independent Video and Filmmakers (AIVF) present the second edition of *The AIVF Guide to Film and Video Distributors*. We felt it was critical to publish this new guide, given how dramatically the media landscape has altered since it was last published in 1990. Since that time, it has been widely utilized by independent makers throughout the country.

AIVF/FIVF has a commitment to collect, organize, and disseminate information that helps to create opportunities for independent media producers. We do this in a number of ways: through our ongoing advocacy efforts, our popular magazine, *The Independent Film and Video Monthly*, our resource library, workshops and seminars, and through our book publication program. In addition to *The AIVF Guide to Film and Video Distributors*, this fall we are also pleased to publish new editions of *The AIVF Guide to International Film and Video Festivals* and *The Next Step: Distributing Independent Films and Videos*. Taken together, these three volumes create a comprehensive library of distribution resources.

We would like to thank Kathryn Bowser, the author of *The Distributors Guide*, for her diligent work on this important publication. I want to especially thank Pamela Calvert, Director of Programs and Services, for her tireless efforts to ensure the most accurate and complete information possible; our designer, Daniel Christmas; and our proofreader, Graham Leggat.

We hope you find this volume helpful, and would appreciate hearing from you as we plan both for its next edition, and for other future AIVF/FIVF publications.

—Ruby Lerner
   Executive Director, AIVF/FIVF
   Winter 1996

imply put, film and video distribution is the process by which a production reaches its intended audience. In reality, the business of distribution is a complex process that is rapidly changing as new technology, audience tastes and options, international possibilities, and range of new works emerge as factors in distribution decisions. For independent producers, it is important to be aware of the players in the field and what impact the business of distribution will have on their productions.

The AIVF Guide to Film and Video Distributors, first conceived nearly a decade ago, is designed to give producers and others in the field an overview of opportunities available to them. Distribution is a volatile business. Since the first publication of the directory, scores of distributors have gone out of business, and new companies have been established to take advantage of the changing landscape in theatrical exhibition, television programming needs, home video, and ancillary consumer arenas.

This guide is based on the results of a questionnaire sent to a database of over 400 commercial and non-profit distributors throughout the United States. The capsule profiles in this book are based on the responses we received from distributors giving us current information on their companies; a limited few contain current information available to us from other sources. Descriptions are of varying lengths; the amount of information on each company is a result of the information provided by the companies. These are not critical analyses of the companies or of the distribution process. For an excellent resource on distribution itself, check out the newly updated AIVF/FIVF companion publication *The Next Step: Distributing Independent Films and Videos*, which discusses different angles of distribution from various professional viewpoints, and covers what to look for in a distributor, promotion, theatrical and non-theatrical markets, television distribution, contracts, self-distribution, and much more. Armed with this information, mediamakers can ask intelligent questions when approaching any of the companies listed in this guide.

The AIVF Guide to Film and Video Distributors contains brief individual company profiles, in alphabetical order. These capsule descriptions are followed by a listing of distribution company names and addresses, a list which includes both the profiled companies and others from which we didn't receive a response but which are presumably still in business as of this writing. In updating this guide, I found that nearly 30% of the addresses had changed from the previous *Distributors Guide* published in 1990. Please keep that in mind when searching for these distributors. Following the addresses is a breakdown of the listed companies by broad categories. We have also added two essay contributions that provide useful information and perspectives on aspects of distribution.

One of the most important things a mediamaker can realize is the importance of thinking about distribution at the early stages of production rather than after completion. Outside of the fact that some distributors may provide pre-production support or completion financing, the distributor is a critical partner in the success or failure of a production to reach its audience. In approaching a distributor, there are perhaps hundreds of issues to consider. These are some of them:

Once you have decided not to go the route of self-distribution, consider the track records of the distributors you approach. Check with other mediamakers who have placed their work with them, look for evidence of their promotional successes in the marketplace, study the quality of their catalogs or other materials, ask about their mailing lists and other resources. See if they have handled risky or innovative productions in a risky and innovative way. See if the company's collection of titles bears some resemblance to your production. Ask questions to determine the distributor's level of expertise in executing suc-cessful campaigns. Find out the company's areas of specialty and see if they conform to your needs. Ask about the relationships the company has with the relevant exhibitors or buyers. Use judgment in determining the nature of your "fit." A smaller, new company may pay more attention to your production and think of more creative, grassroots distribution strategies than a mini-major, which, on the other hand, may have more resources, financial and otherwise, to commit to your project.

Most film and video makers are intimately familiar with production, story ideas, character, art, direction, etc., but are not necessarily aware of the market forces that shape what will happen with the completed work. That is the distributor's job. Generally, a distributor will be responsible for bookings with exhibitors, revenue collection, marketing, advertising, promotion and publicity campaigns, sales, audience development, and the creation of promotional materials such as catalogs and brochures, one-sheets, trailers, commercials, and ad slicks. Therefore, the relationship you have with a distributor who understands the nature of your work and the market for it is an important element in its success. The distributor should have an overall level of enthusiasm for the work and be willing to give it a special creative push. The company should have established relationships with the market you are trying to reach; a distributor of major feature films has different modes of operation than a distributor of video art. Understand the nature of your work and have realistic expectations for it.

Be aware of what a distributor will need from the producer. Perhaps one of the most overlooked needs is the importance of good stills (color and black-and-white) taken during production. After a distributor generates a buzz about the production and has newspapers and trade journals interested and ready to write about it, it really hurts to have only fuzzy, non-relevant stills for publication. Other items that the producer may need to provide include lab access letters, publicity materials and any existing press reviews, film prints, cassettes (NTSC and

PAL), music cue sheets, M&E tracks, 1" NTSC masters, bios of principal crew and cast, copyright verifications, warranties of ownership, scripts, and festival and award listings. Some of these deliverables will be outlined in the contract with the distributor.

In negotiating that contract, a good entertainment attorney is necessary. The essay by Mark Litwak in this guide details some contract points that producers should consider. Generally, producers should be aware of what rights will be made available to the distributor (whether they will be exclusive or non-exclusive, for example, whether they will be for all territories and markets, or whether the distributor will be responsible for licensing such rights). Theatrical distributors, for example, may retain rights to video, television or non-theatrical markets to capitalize on the momentum created by a successful theatrical release. Determine the financial commitment the distributor will make to prints, tapes, advertising, and other costs; which costs are to be shared between the producer and distributor; and timetables for release. Astute and reliable financial recordkeeping and reporting is essential to the relationship, of course, so that should be spelled out, along with any advances, guarantees and other financial arrangements. Each deal is different, depending upon the type of production and the commitments on both sides—a theatrical motion picture will have different issues to be resolved than a non-theatrical short documentary aimed at high school audiences. *Generally*, however, the distributor will cover such up-front expenses as promotion, printing, shipping, film/tape duplication, etc., and will determine exhibitor costs and percentages. These expenses will be deducted from the total revenue generated, and the producer and distributor will split remaining revenues based on an agreed percentage. Payments may be made quarterly or semi-annually. An attorney can help with determining appropriate contractual elements concerning accounting, reporting, and so on.

Marketing and promotion are the linchpins of the work of media distribution. A good distributor will be aware of market forces as they relate to the productions they acquire.

Non-theatrical distributors should be familiar with the rental and purchasing needs and capabilities of libraries, government agencies, film societies, museums, schools and universities, media centers, health institutions and community groups, and how to reach them. A good customer database and/or access to mailing lists are critical. Relationships forged at festivals, conventions, professional meetings, and industry events are also important. Materials should reflect the quality of understanding of the distributor's library. Check out whether the catalog is well designed, and whether it gives each production space and context. Some distributors prepare packages of related work for marketing impact, or prepare special one-sheets or brochures highlighting exceptional works. Rental and sales policies on prices, payments, shipping, etc., should be clearly explained, firm and enforceable. Unless the production has fully exploited the festival circuit prior to acquisition, the distributor should be a partner in determining a festival strategy. And the distributor should be aware of new technological opportunities for media delivery.

With more and more options for entertainment and the dominance of huge studio-financed multi million-dollar marketing campaigns for major commercial releases, the theatrical distributor should be keenly aware of the markets for the films it acquires and how to reach those markets. Special screenings, word-of-mouth publicity campaigns, special press campaigns, creative advertising, cast/crew tours, image design, and a host of other approaches must be carefully planned and executed to get audiences into the theaters. It helps if the distributor can identify and reach non-traditional or underserved markets.

In general, producers should continually be aware of the distribution company's strengths and weaknesses in all of the above areas, and make a decision based on the character and reliability of the company. Ask questions, engage expert help, and consider what is best for your particular production.

Good luck!

I would like to acknowledge the following: Ruby Lerner, AIVF/FIVF executive director and Pamela Calvert, AIVF/FIVF project coordinator for this publication, both of whose tenacity made this book possible; the distribution companies which took time from their busy schedules to respond to the questionnaire; the AIVF/FIVF staff, including Johnny McNair, information specialist, Laura D. Davis, advertising sales director, and other staff and interns who assisted with the arduous process of producing and mailing questionnaires.

— Kathryn Bowser
   Winter 1996

A-PIX/UNAPIX ENTERTAINMENT, INC.

500 Fifth Avenue, 46th Floor
New York, NY 10110
Telephone: (212) 764-7171
Fax: (212) 575-6578

Unapix Entertainment is a publicly traded company whose core business is the international licensing of its collection of television programs and feature films. The company's A-Pix division releases about 24 titles annually into theatrical, home video and television markets. Its publicly traded parent company, Unapix Entertainment, buys finished features for worldwide sales. It is launching a completion fund for features in progress. Many of A-Pix's releases go straight to video, cable and pay-per-view.

Year established: 1994

Area(s) of specialty: Theatrical distribution of fiction features

Company officers: David Fox, president, Robert Baruch, president (Unapix Films), Paul Davis-Miller, vice president, acquisitions (Unapix), Amy Moore, vice president, production (Unapix), Alicia Reilly, director of acquisitions (A-Pix)

Contact: Alicia Reilly

ABC DISTRIBUTION COMPANY

825 Seventh Avenue, 5th floor
New York, NY 10019
Telephone: (212) 456-1725
Fax: (212) 456-1708

ABC Distribution Company currently handles over 200 titles, including features, documentaries, animated, classic films, sports, musical and artistic programs. The company distributes to all media in the theatrical, television and home video markets on a worldwide basis. Publicity for its collection is provided in-house; special promotions with reviews, announcements, special brochures, and paid advertising are developed for various programs. Overseas subdistributors are also used. Sales representatives attend MIP-COM, Monte Carlo, MIP-TV, Cannes Film Festival, AFM, MIFED, as well as other markets to introduce new acquisitions. Some titles in its collection include *Cabaret*; *Dangerous Indiscretion*; *Someone Else's Child*; *Double Cross*; *Ebbtide*; *The Magic Flute* (children); *The Secret Garden* (animated); *The Amy Fisher Story*; *Stolen Babies*; *Rebecca*; *Spellbound*; *Intermezzo*; *Notes for My Daughter* (afterschool special); *Spring Fling*; *Family Reunion*; *A Relative Nightmare*; *The Real Frankenstein: An Untold Story*; *World of Discovery* (documentary series); *Prizzi's Honor*; *Silkwood*; *Young Doctors in Love*; *They Shoot Horses, Don't They?*; *Bitter Blood* (mini-series); *Whose Child Is This?*; *The War For Baby Jessica*. The parent company is ABC Cable and International Broadcast, Inc. In addition to the New York office listed above, other offices are: Sales Office, 77 West 66th Street, 17th Floor, New York, NY 10023, (212) 456-7428, fax: (212) 456-7570, West Coast Office, 2040

Avenue of the Stars, 2nd Floor, Century City, CA 90067; (310) 557-7111; fax: (310) 557-7925.

Year established: 1979

Area(s) of specialty: Varied

Company officers: Joseph Y. Abrams, president, Jeremiah G. Sullivan, senior vice president-finance and administration, Michael J. Dragotto, vice president-international theatrical and home video sales, Maria D. Komodikis, vice president-international television sales, Carol A. Brokaw, vice president-advertising, sales administration and operations

Number of employees: 70

Contact: Joseph Y. Abrams

ADLER MEDIA

6849 Old Dominion Drive, Suite 360
McLean, VA 22101
Telephone: (703) 556-8880
Fax: (703) 556-9288

Adler Media distributes documentaries on such topics as travel, adventure, history, music, entertainment, children, science, military history, aviation, short subjects, and the environment. It is looking for high quality documentaries with voice-over narration (no hosts). Some examples of the 200+ hours of programming in its collection are *Swiss Railway Journeys; Alaska Outdoors; Elite Fighting Forces; Rock Revolutions; The World of Sharks and Barracuda; Crazy Inventions; British Rail Journeys;* and *Animals of the Bible.* Adler distributes to an international market and to television and home video, and welcomes submissions from independent producers. Contracts are usually exclusive by market (television, home video) and by territory. Representatives attend MIPCOM, Monte Carlo, MIP, NATPE, and AFM, with stands at the first three.

Year established: 1981

Area(s) of specialty: Documentaries

Company officers: Larry Adler

Number of employees: 5

Contact: Larry Adler

JAMES AGEE FILM PROJECT

316 East Main Street
Johnson City, TN 37601
Telephone: (615) 926-8637
Fax: (804) 971-2921

The James Agee Film Project is a small non-profit film organization which distributes a collection of prize-winning films that it has produced to the non-theatrical market; it also plans to distribute a number of other producers. Its focus is feature documentaries, and it is seeking southern regional productions. Its films cover a variety of issues: history, literature, religion, social justice, environment, energy, politics and peace.

Year established: 1974

Area(s) of specialty: Documentaries

Company officers: Ross Spears, John Roach

Number of employees: 8

Contact: Dale Moore

AIMS MEDIA

9710 DeSoto Avenue
Chatsworth, CA 91311
Telephone: (818) 773-4300/(800) 367-2467
Fax: (818) 376-6405

AIMS Media, a diversified non-theatrical distributor, has a library of over 1,000 titles of educational films and videos. Each year, it releases nearly 100 new works while actively promoting its existing library; new releases are included in a catalog supplement as well as promoted via release sheets, and separate catalogs are prepared in various subject areas (e.g., safety and health, law enforcement). The company specializes in the curriculum needs of public and private schools (preschool to university level), information needs of library patrons and researchers, training films and videos for industrial and governmental use, and "how to" and informational works for the general public. Its catalog lists works in the language arts, English and humanities, social studies, science, mathematics, art and music, computers and technology, vocational education, physical education, health and guidance, safety education, crime prevention, substance abuse, driver education, and training and development.Some programs are packaged in series, and AIMS also prepares discussion and study guides. Representatives attend MIPCOM and AFM, as well as international, national and regional conventions.

Year established: 1957

Area(s) of specialty: Non-theatrical distribution

ALTERNATIVE VIDEOS

P.O. Box 270797
Dallas, TX 75227
Telephone: (214) 823-6030

Alternative Videos is a video mail order company and store which focuses on videos by or about people of African descent. It has an African-American Cinematique Club for mail order renters.

Area(s) of specialty: African-American videos

Company officers: Beverly DeBase

Contact: Beverly DeBase

ALTSCHUL GROUP CORPORATION

1560 Sherman Avenue, Suite 100
Evanston, IL 60201
Telephone: (708) 328-6700
Fax: (708) 328-6706
e-mail: agcmedia@starnet.nc.com

Altschul Group Corporation is a leading distributor of educational media, with 4,000 titles in its library and 2,500 active titles. These titles are offered to more than 3,000 customers worldwide. The company distributes videos, laserdiscs, and CD-ROM titles to schools, libraries, health departments, business, industry and many other markets, including patient education. Its focus is educational videos for the K-12 curriculum, and special-interest titles for public libraries. It is looking for high-production-quality works with an ethnic mix; no talking heads. Some of the titles in its collection are *Southeast Asia Today Series*; *New Parent Series*; *Smart Snacking for Children*; *Immunizations: What Lily Learned*; *Domestic Violence and Young Adults*; *Mexico Today*; and *Mathica's Mathshop*.

Year established: 1945

Area(s) of specialty: Educational videos

Company officers: Joe Farragher, president, Joel Altschul, chairman

Number of employees: 45

Contact: Jim McCall, Margaret Dugan

AMAZING MOVIES

7471 Melrose Avenue, Suite 7
Los Angeles, CA 90046
Telephone: (213) 852-1396
Fax: (213) 658-7265

Amazing Movies' specialty is worldwide feature film distribution, and television and home video distribution, and it is "one of the leading proponents of American independent filmmaking in the international marketplace." The company initially earned its reputation in the action and horror genres, and has diversified to include several types of films. With over 150 titles in its library, the company is looking for films which are visually interesting, since much of its distribution activity is international. It has also developed its art house market, with the theatrical release of films such as *Mask of Desire*; *At Ground Zero*; *Natural Born Crazies*; and *Under Heat*. Amazing Movies has a strategic alliance with the Rapid Film Group, which has launched a new venture devoted to critically acclaimed, cutting-edge, U.S. independent films, *The Best of the New American Underground Cinema*, which have not received international distribution outside of the festival circuit. Some of the titles in that collection are *Mod Fuck Explosion*; *I Don't Hate Las Vegas Anymore*; *The Great Unpleasantness*; *Shameless*; *Second Cousin Once Removed*; *Steal America*; and *Begotten*. The company

represents more than 75 feature films for major independent producers.
Year established: 1984
Area(s) of specialty: Feature films
Company officers: Douglas Witkins, president, Xochitl Ruiz, director of operations
Number of employees: 6
Contact: Tymme Reitz, manager of sales and acquisitions

AMBROSE VIDEO PUBLISHING, INC.
28 West 44th St., #2100
New York, NY 10036
Telephone: (212) 768-7373
Fax: (212) 768-9282

Ambrose Video Publishing, Inc., handles documentary features and shorts, educational videos, and health, medical and scientific works. Many titles are training videos (stress management, workplace literacy, management skills, health, etc.). It acquires works primarily through working with broadcasters, independent producers and screenings, and currently has about 750 titles in its collection. The company distributes worldwide to the non-theatrical and home video markets, utilizing sales agents in foreign countries. The company distributes programs produced by CBS, BBC, A&E, Discovery, PBS and HBO. Titles include *LifeStories: Families in Crisis* series; *Connections 2*; *Body Atlas*; *Great Commanders*; and *Over America*.
Year established: 1987
Area(s) of specialty: Educational and training programs
Company officers: William Ambrose, president, Kathy Popolani, vice president-finance
Number of employees: 35
Contact: William Ambrose

ANGELIKA FILMS
110 Greene Street, Suite 1102
New York, NY 10012
Telephone: (212) 274-1990
Fax: (212) 966-4957

Angelika Films distributes independent narrative features, documentary features, and animated films. Each film is carefully nurtured. Angelika was founded to represent pickup acquisitions and low-budget features in pre-production, and seeks films for theatrical release, preferably with worldwide rights available; it also distributes non-theatrically, to home video and laser disc, all television, and in all territories. Angelika International is its in-house foreign sales company. The company also opened the Angelika Film Center in downtown New York in late 1989; it is a complete six-plex which showcases many of the film company's independent releases along with commercial and innovative films. Its titles include *The Trial* and *Resistance*.

Year established: 1985

Area(s) of specialty: Feature film distribution and exhibition

Company officers: Eva Saleh, president, Angelika Films, Jessica Saleh Hunt, president, Angelika Film Center, Angelika Saleh, chairman, Jeffrey Jacobs, film buyer, Rafael Guadalupe, vice president, business affairs.

Contact: Eva Saleh

APPALSHOP FILM AND VIDEO

306 Madison Street
Whitesburg, KY 41858
Telephone: (606) 633-0108
Fax: (606) 633-1009
e-mail: appalshop@aol.com

Appalshop, a media arts center, distributes documentary features, shorts and television projects produced by Appalshop film and video makers; producers are the distributors. In its 25-year history, Appalshop has produced over 82 documentary films reflecting the experiences of living in the Appalachian mountains and in rural America. Some of the films and videos in its collection include *Fast Food Women* (women in the work force); *Belinda* (AIDS); *Chemical Valley* (environmental pollution); *Justice in the Coalfields* (labor); *Strangers & Kin* (stereotyping of the Appalachian people); *Morgan Sexton* (profiles the music and lifestyle of Appalachian people).

Year established: 1969

Area(s) of specialty: Documentaries—social, environmental, women, labor, and regional issues

Company officers: Dee Davis, executive producer

Number of employees: 32

Contact: Carolyn Sturgill

ARROW ENTERTAINMENT, INC.

One Rockefeller Plaza, 16th Floor
New York, NY 10020
Telephone: (212) 332-8140
Fax: (212) 332-8161

Arrow Entertainment is an independent film distribution and production company, comprised of several wholly-owned subsidiaries. The company distributes feature-length films and documentaries in several markets; its operations focus on U.S. theatrical, home video, television and non-theatrical distribution and foreign theatrical, home video and television sales. Arrow is also involved in the development and production of independent features, and is looking to acquire television series. In the U.S. theatrical market, Arrow specializes in American independent and foreign films; in the home video market it also distributes genre titles. Some of the sixty titles in its library include *Bandit Queen; Ermo; The Wooden Man's Bride; Homage; Farmer & Chase; One Way Out; 301 302; Condition Red; Gumby: The Movie; Sofie; My Life's in Turnaround; Combination Platter; Abducted II: The Reunion.* Representatives attend Cannes, MIFED, AFM, MIPCOM, MIP-ASIA, and NATPE.

Year established: 1992

Area(s) of specialty: Independent distribution and production

Company officers: Dennis Friedland, president, Jason Blum, vice president, acquisitions, Steve Fagan, national sales manager, Sridhar Sreekakula, vice president, worldwide sales

Number of employees: 17

Contact: Jason Blum

ARTISTIC LICENSE FILMS

470 Park Avenue South, 9th Floor
New York, NY 10016
Telephone: (212) 251-8718
Fax: (212) 251-8606
e-mail: artlic@aol.com

Artistic License Films "bridges the gap between self-distribution and distribution," providing "independent filmmakers, producers and distribution companies with individualized services to ensure the theatrical release of a film." Featuring many films of women's interest, gay interest and Jewish interest, the catalog includes documentaries, comedies and political thrillers from throughout the world, all of which are independent films. With fifteen films in distribution, Artistic License boasts such independent works as *Jupiter's Wife; She Lives to Ride; The Last Klezmer; Dallas Doll; The Jar; Manhattan By Numbers; Resistance; Rock Hudson's Home Movies* and *Central Park.* Dealing exclusively with theatrical releases, the company makes service deals through booking agents; films tend to be booked in calendar houses, both to keep advertising costs down and to maintain low-risk bookings that will make a profit.

Year established: 1994

Area(s) of specialty: Features, documentaries

Company officers: Sande Zeig, president

Number of employees: 2

Contact: Sande Zeig

ATA TRADING CORPORATION

50 West 34th Street, Suite 5C6
New York, NY 10001
Telephone: (212) 594-6460
Fax: (212) 594-6461

ATA Trading Corporation currently handles 200 titles and series, including such works as *The New South Africa: A Personal Journey; Playing for Peace; Blood Ties: The Life and Work of Sally Mann; Lazy Man's Zen; Mr. Ahmed; An American Affair; Chicago Blues Jam; The Other Side of Nashville; Meats & Jesus; River Invaders: The Scourge of Zebra Mussels;* and *Kissy Cousins.* It handles all types of programs, with no specialty, and looks for programs that would have a general audience appeal to all ages. It is actively seeking new types of films and videos to handle, including fiction and documentary features and shorts, educational, video, arts, animated, sports, health/medical/scientific and music works. ATA Trading Corporation acquires films from personal recommendation, screenings, markets, and submissions from independent producers. It has representatives in major countries who keep it up to date on their needs. The company contracts exclusively for domestic and foreign theatrical, non-theatrical, television and home video markets, and also acts as a foreign sales agent. Publicity is done out of house. ATA is open to discussing scripts and treatments and offering advice on improving chances of distribution. Some funds may be available for co-productions.

Year established: 1947

Area(s) of specialty: General

Company officers: Harold G. Lewis, president, Susan Lewis, vice president

Number of employees: 3

Contact: Hal Lewis, Susan Lewis

BARR MEDIA GROUP

P.O. Box 7878
12801 Schabarum Avenue
Irwindale, CA 91706-7878
Telephone: (818) 338-7878/(800) 234-7878
Fax: (818) 814-2672

Barr Media's catalog lists over 1,500 titles aimed at the international non-theatrical, curriculum-based educational market. The company seeks out a broad range of subjects for K-12 and college markets. Programs under 30 minutes are preferred, and longer works are considered for television. Subject areas cover English/language arts (literature on film, guidance, study skills, holiday films), foreign language skills, communication, social studies (history, energy/ecology, geography, economics, career, human behavior), science and mathematics (scientific methods, life/physical/earth/space sciences), health and safety (alcohol/drug education, special needs, nutrition/health, safety, mental health, physical education), music and art. Separate catalogs advertise health education films/videos and management training films and videos. The company employs sales representatives covering national regions, and sub-distributors are also located in Australia, Canada, Puerto Rico, Singapore, Spain and UK. Barr accepts submissions from independent producers and works with contract producers, as well as attending film festivals and AFM.

Year established: 1937

Area(s) of specialty: Educational media

Company officers: Don Barr, president

Number of employees: 50

Contact: George Holland, executive vice president

BAXLEY MEDIA GROUP

110 West Main Street
Urbana, IL 61801-2700
Telephone: (217) 384-4838
Fax: (217) 384-8280

Baxley Media Group distributes films and videos on health-related topics, such as aging, AIDS, eating disorders, women's and children's health, ethics, death and dying, patient education and special education. There are over 100 titles in its library. While it is primarily a non-theatrical distributor, it is open to opportunities in television which will benefit the company and the producer. It contracts both exclusively and non-exclusively. All publicity is done in-house by Baxley Media Group staff, including special release brochures, topic area brochures (e.g., AIDS, ethics, eating disorders, etc.), occasional display advertising, conference showings and exhibits and directory listings. Presently, the company distributes to the U.S., Canada, Australia, New Zealand, Hong Kong, Singapore, Taiwan and U.K.. Some examples of titles include *Living With AIDS; Heavy Load; Thin Dreams; Fools' Dance*; and *One Step Ahead*. Although its specialization is health-related titles, advertising is not limited to health markets; mailings go to hospitals, colleges, nursing and medical schools, nursing homes, high schools and professional associations.

Year established: 1983

Area(s) of specialty: Health care and human relations

Company officers: Carolyn Baxley, president, Karen Krusa, director of operations

Number of employees: 5

Contact: Carolyn Baxley

BULLFROG FILMS

Box 149
Oley, PA 19547
Telephone: (610) 779-8226/(800) 543-FROG
Fax: (610) 370-1978
e-mail: bullfrog@igc.apc.org

Bullfrog Films, one of the country's leading distributors of programs on the environment, handles over 500 international works which exhibit concern about and commitment to environmental issues (broadly defined, including development, energy, agriculture, nutrition, indigenous peoples, and women's issues) and performing arts. It is helpful if programs are under 30 minutes long, and are appropriate to the K-12 curriculum. Bullfrog's library includes documentary features and shorts, animated works, television productions, arts programs, and educational films and videos in many subject areas, including ecology and environment, forests, genetics, marine biology, animal studies, energy, agriculture, children's programs, development and global issues, economics, future studies, women's studies, native peoples, waste management, arts and the humanities. The company consistently searches for videos and interactive programs on any aspect of the environment, and specifically seeks out works aimed at very young children. All of the more than 500 titles in Bullfrog's collection are currently in distribution, and include such titles as *The Decade of Destruction; Blowpipes and Bulldozers; Developing Stories; Kanehsatake; Toast; Banana; Banana, Banana Slugs!; OWL/TV; F.R.O.G.; Green Animation; A Celebration of Birds; Concerto for the Earth; Making a Difference; Ravel; Guitar; World Drums; My War Years: Arnold Schoenberg; Masterclass with Menuhin;* and *When Abortion Was Illegal: Untold Stories.* Bullfrog will take on programs which may not be hugely financially successful, but which contain information that it believes should be released. The company also welcomes early consultation, will look at works-in-progress, and urges producers to consult with a teacher so that Bullfrog can pinpoint the program's position in the curriculum. It also urges producers to consider making 20-30 minute versions while editing, to conform to classroom requirements. Acquisitions are sought from independent producers, festivals, and markets. Bullfrog's primary market is nontheatrical, with the importance of its theatrical market growing as it acquires more feature-length films. As a result of growing environmental concern, its semi-theatrical market is expanding, as are cable television sales. Representatives attend several film festivals and markets each year, including INCITE, American Library Association, and National Educational Media Network. The company considers festivals very important to raising a program's profile, and if the program has foreign television possibilities, it is entered in many foreign festivals; alternatively, if Bullfrog feels that any new environmental film needs to be seen, it will also enter it. The company distributes its programs nationwide and to Canada, Australia/New Zealand, Hong Kong, Taiwan, Singapore, Malaysia, and South Korea; foreign markets for television sales are very important. Video-on-demand and specialized cable channels are just starting to become important to Bullfrog. It also has a network of independent representatives who call on customers directly; they see all new releases and Bullfrog explains the selling points of each title. Besides the regular trade journals (*Booklist, Library Journal,* etc.), Bullfrog also sends review copies to special interest magazines based on the program's content. It will also assist producers in premiering new programs in their own cities. Target audiences are K-12, colleges and universities, public libraries, government agencies, and home video for the right title; the company maintains an extensive customer list as its most important resource. Bullfrog's basic contractual agreement is exclusive U.S. non-theatrical rights, with a window of at least 3 years in which there will be no home video release unless through the company. Most contracts are on a standard royalty basis, but in a very few cases it has given advances against future royalties. All other rights are negotiable. Bullfrog has had success with programs where the producer has been willing to appear with the program, and has also had success with a three-tiered pricing policy.

Year established: 1973

Area(s) of specialty: Environment, performing arts

Company officers: John Hoskyns-Abrahall, Winifred Scherrer, partners

Number of employees: 7 plus 10 sales reps working on commission

Contact: John Hoskyns-Abrahall

BUREAU FOR AT-RISK YOUTH

645 New York Avenue
Huntington, NY 11743
Telephone: (516) 673-4584
Fax: (516) 673-4544

The Bureau for At-Risk Youth distributes, among other educational materials, educational and guidance-oriented videos in such areas as parenting education/involvement, drug-free schools and communities, violence prevention for safe schools, gangs, staff development/in-service training, character and life skills education, and cultural diversity. There are about 200 titles in its collection. Primary audiences are schools, juvenile justice agencies, and social organizations. Distribution of its videos is via direct mail catalogs to niche markets. It will offer advances against royalties, and will also look at works-in-progress and rough cuts.

Year established: 1991

Area(s) of specialty: Education, at-risk youth

Company officers: Edward Werz, president

Contact: Sally Germain, Edward Werz

CALIFORNIA NEWSREEL

149 Ninth Street, Suite 420
San Francisco, CA 94103
Telephone: (415) 621-6196
Fax: (415) 621-6522
e-mail: newsreel@ix.netcom.com

California Newsreel, a non-profit educational distributor, is one of the country's oldest independent documentary film distributors, with a particularly strong collection of films on Africa, including South Africa, films on African-American life and history, and films on the media. It acquires films across genres primarily for the college, high school and public library markets, looking specifically for films which can be used to illustrate key curricular points, films "which rise above their particularities to provide a larger conceptual framework." The largest audiences for its films are students, media arts center audiences and community groups. California Newsreel handles narrative and documentary features and shorts for domestic distribution to non-theatrical (primary market), semi-theatrical (an "increasingly limited market"), home video ("increasingly important both as an arena for reaching individuals with special interests and institutions"), and television markets. California Newsreel currently has about 100 titles in its collection, with 45 in active distribution. Its Southern Africa Media Center houses several works, and it also includes a Southern Africa Video Library to enable institutions to build core Southern African curricula and a collection of several films on African-American history. California Newsreel specializes in focused distribution or niche marketing, offering special package discounts for multiple title purchases and extensive "co-marketing" with professional and advocacy groups. It also puts together resource guides and program series to enhance the messages conveyed in its film collection. It tries to identify productions while they are in production from scanning lists of grants and encourages submissions from independent producers, as well as an occasional festival acquisition. The company will make advances against royalties, preferably during post-production, but has in the past committed itself to films at earlier stages of production. Some examples of titles in its collection are *Ethnic Notions; Color Adjustment; Black Is...Black Ain't; James Baldwin: The Price of the Ticket; Richard Wright-Black Boy; Berkeley in the 60s; Yeelen; Hyenas;* and *La Vie Est Belle.*

Year established: 1968

Area(s) of specialty: Media studies, African cinema, African-American history and culture, literature

Company officers: Lawrence Daressa, Laurence Adelman, Cornelius Moore, co-directors

Number of employees: 5

Contact: Lawrence Daressa

CAMBRIDGE DOCUMENTARY FILMS

P.O. Box 385
Cambridge, MA 02139
Telephone: (617) 354-3677
Fax: (617) 899-9602

Cambridge Documentary Films is a non-profit filmmaking and distribution organization; its goal "has been to create provocative and controversial films that challenge audiences to think and act on important social issues." The company handles documentary shorts, educational films and videos, and programs dealing with women's issues. It is currently working with twelve titles, including *Life's Work; Not Just a Job;* Academy Award-winner *Defending Our Lives; The Last Empire; Still Killing Us Softly: Advertising's Image of Women; Advertising Alcohol; Choosing Children; Hazardous Inheritance; Pink Triangles;* and *Rape Culture.* Works from independent producers are accepted. Study guides are made available with some programs. Target audiences are primarily non-theatrical.

Year established: 1974

Area(s) of specialty: Social issues

Company officers: Carol Belding, president, Joan Sawyer, treasurer, Ellen Shub, secretary

Number of employees: 5

Contact: Margaret Lazarus, Renner Wunderlich

ARTHUR CANTOR FILMS, INC.

1501 Broadway, Suite 403
New York, NY 10036
Telephone: (212) 391-2650
Fax: (212) 391-2677

Arthur Cantor Films, Inc., specializes in literary, theatrical and dance subjects, plus ethnic societies (Jewish themes, films about India, Native American and Inuit societies, etc.), distributed to home video, non-theatrical, and theatrical markets, as well as public and cable television. Acquisition is primarily through submissions; libraries, schools and sell-through venues are the major target markets. Some titles in its collection are *Akropolis; At the Crossroads: Jews in Eastern Europe Today; We Were So Beloved; Almonds and Raisins; The Golden Age of Second Avenue; Inughuit; Homage to Chagall; A Jumpin' Night in the Garden of Eden; Partisans of Vilna; The Rise and Fall of the Borscht Belt; Turkey's Sephardim: 500 Years; Weapons of the Spirit; Jan Peerce: If I Were A Rich Man; Memories of Berlin: Twilight of Weimar Culture; The Private World of Lewis Carroll; Jewish Soul Music: The Art of Giora Feidman; Ansel Adams: Photographer.*

Year established: 1968

Area(s) of specialty: Theater arts, Jewish theme documentary films.

Company officers: Arthur Cantor

Contact: Arthur Cantor

CANYON CINEMA

2325 Third Street, Suite 338
San Francisco, CA 94107
Telephone: (415) 626-2255

Canyon Cinema is a "no-profit" cooperative distribution center for independent filmmakers and is one of the principal sources of independent cinema. Its encyclopedic catalog lists well over 3500 16mm and super 8 titles from hundreds of international filmmakers, representing a history of the independent filmmaking movement from the 1950s through the present; yearly catalog supplements are published. There are no restrictions on form, content or length; animation, documentary, experimental/art films, erotic, narrative, shorts, etc. are in the catalog. The company was established as a cooperative 30 years ago by a small number of filmmakers who felt the need for an alternative to the existing distribution structure. Canyon Cinema is a membership organization, which any filmmaker may join by paying a yearly membership fee (which goes toward publishing the catalog and updates and operating expenses) and depositing work. Members write their own catalog descriptions and establish their own rental fees. Members collect the majority of the rental fee and the prints remain the filmmakers' property. It is Canyon's policy not to promote any one film over another but to promote the overall organization, and it will not act as a subdistributor for films not made by members. Members are encouraged to promote their own work and develop thematic packages of films that can be advertised and rented together. Canyon distributes videos of titles currently in film form which have been placed with the company for distribution; videos are accepted for sale only. It also handles rentals of installation pieces in which the major component is film or video. Rentals paid to Canyon Cinema are credited to the filmmakers' accounts, with a percentage of 65% to filmmakers, 35% to Canyon, with accounting provided only on request. Film sales royalties are 85% to filmmaker and 15% to Canyon; video sales royalties are 75% filmmaker, 25% Canyon.

Year established: 1966

Area(s) of specialty: Independent cinema

Contact: Distribution manager

CAPITAL COMMUNICATIONS

P.O. Box 3459
Venice, FL 34293
Telephone: (800) 822-5678

Capital Communications has 600 titles in its collection and currently handles 50-60. Its catalog features films on adventure, health, and safety, and the company accepts documentary features and shorts, educational, video, arts, animated, sports, health/medical/scientific and television works. Distribution is to non-theatrical venues and television (public, network and cable), worldwide and contracted exclusively. Representatives attend Monte Carlo and MIP-TV.

Year established: 1966

Area(s) of specialty: General titles

Number of employees: 6

Contact: James Springer

CAROUSEL FILM AND VIDEO

260 Fifth Avenue, Suite 405
New York, NY 10001
Telephone: (212) 683-1660
Fax: (212) 683-1662

Carousel Film and Video specializes in documentaries and shorts for the non-theatrical market in the U.S. and Canada, specifically programs in the 12-28 minute range. With over 250 titles in its catalog, the company handles a wide subject range, such as African-American/Black studies, art, biography/profiles, business and industry, children's programming, social concerns, environment, guidance/values, history, international issues, language arts, literary adaptations, multicultural/contemporary ethnic studies, parent/child relations, politics and government, prejudice, psychology, social studies, sociology, special needs, substance abuse/addiction, and travel. Target audiences include schools, public libraries, universities, business, industry, and government. Some new releases include *The Civil Rights Rap; Ida B. Wells; Royal Federal Blues; Harry Crews: Guilty as Charged; Warren Oates: Across the Border; The First Christmas; Lit'l Boy Grown; Peace and Quiet; Surviving the Family; The War Zone; The Two-Hundred Dollar "Willie Mays;" The Big Gig; Color of Justice; Harlem Renaissance: The Black Poets; Just School; Last Breeze of Summer; Africa Calls: Its Drums and Musical Instruments; African Art and Sculpture; Tuskegee Airmen; Children With a Dream; Jihad; White Boys Can't Dance; The Silver Maiden; Children of the Dust; Jennifer's Chinese Diary; Jenny; Are You My Mother;* and *A Little Vicious*. The catalog also includes several series and collections, including an extensive listing of programs from CBS and a series of productions from the American Film Institute (including first films of many independent directors).

Year established: 1958

Area(s) of specialty: Educational, non-theatrical distribution

Company officers: David B. Dash, president, Michael A. Dash, vice president

Number of employees: 4

Contact: Michael A. Dash

CASTLE HILL PRODUCTIONS

1414 Avenue of the Americas
New York, NY 10019
Telephone: (212) 888-0080
Fax: (212) 644-0956

Castle Hill is a theatrical film distributor, with a wide range of titles. Some recent theatrical releases, some of which were American premieres, have included *A Business Affair; Hotel Sorrento; A Great Day in Harlem; Welles's Othello; Reunion; Two Small Bodies; The Hawk; Becoming Colette; The Silent Touch; The Secret Rapture;* a John Cassavetes Collection; *The Texas*

Chainsaw Massacre; George Stevens: A Filmmaker's Journey; And Nothing But the Truth; Memoirs of A River; and several French comedies.

Area(s) of specialty: Theatrical and semi-theatrical film distribution

Year established: 1978

Contact: Distribution manager

CHURCHILL MEDIA

12210 Nebraska Avenue
Los Angeles, CA 90025
Telephone: (310) 207-6600/(800) 334-7830
Fax: (310) 207-1330

Churchill Media handles films and videos geared to the non-theatrical educational market, specializing in health, children's, and curricula from elementary through college levels as well as social documentary. It sells to schools, public libraries, health agencies, hospitals and colleges. Among the subject areas covered in its catalog are Academy Award winners, adventure, aging, agriculture, animal life, art/filmmaking, biography, books to film, children's films, consumer education, energy, ecology, fairytales/folktales, history, human relations, community studies, mental health, multicultural studies, motivational films, physiology, poetry, sex education, women's studies, values, and sports. The company also distributes internationally to Canada, Australia, Europe, India, and New Zealand, with agents in Europe and India, and sub-distributors in Canada, Australia and New Zealand. Churchill contracts exclusively for non-theatrical distribution, with royalties paid quarterly.

Year established: 1961

Area(s) of specialty: Educational films and videos

Number of employees: 35

Contact: Marilyn Engle

CINEMA CLASSICS

P.O. Box 174
Village Station
New York, NY 10014
Telephone: (212) 675-6692
Fax: (212) 675-6594

Cinema Classics has listings of all genres of films and videos for rent, including suspense, cult, horror, classics, and science fiction.

Area(s) of specialty: Video rentals

THE CINEMA GUILD

1697 Broadway, Suite 506
New York, NY 10019
Telephone: (212) 246-5522
Fax: (212) 246-5525

The Cinema Guild, a leading distributor of independently produced films and videos, celebrated its 20th anniversary in 1995. It offers producers full service distribution in territories worldwide in all markets, including theatrical, semi-theatrical, non-theatrical, television and home video. Founded by filmmakers, the company handles a large number of award-winning works by prominent independent producers, and offers special handling of all of its releases; it distributes shorts, medium-length and feature length films in documentary, fiction and instructional formats. It is most interested in documentary films with multi-disciplinary academic applications. Among the more than 50 titles in The Cinema Guild's library are features such as *The Adventures of Juan Quin Quin; Anarchism in America; The Animals Film; Are We Winning, Mommy?: America and the Cold War; Before Stonewall: The Making of a Gay and Lesbian Community; The Black Banana; Comedienne; Courage of the People; Crime and Punishment; Czech Women: Now We Are Free; Dead End Kids: A Story of Nuclear Power; Delivered Vacant; Escape From China; Halftime: Five Yale Men at Midlife; Harry Bridges: A Man and His Union; Iracema; My Dinner With Abbie; Only Emptiness Remains; Parting of the Ways; Rape/Crisis; Rebellion in Patagonia; Secuestro: A Story of a Kidnapping; Sometimes I Look At My Life; The Tables Turned; Through the Wire*; and *The Traitors*. The collection also includes works in the arts and humanities (architecture and public art, biography, children's and young adult, cinema studies, dance, language arts and literature, music, painting, sculpture, graphic arts, photography), health (AIDS, disabilities, human sexuality, medical science, mental health and psychology, substance abuse), the sciences, social studies (anthropology, Black studies, business and management, Chicano studies, criminal justice, education, family relations, history, labor studies, media studies, Native American studies, political science, Puerto Rican studies, religion, sociology, urban studies, women's studies), and world cultures (African, Asian, Latin American, Mideast, Europe, and other regions). With each acquisition, The Cinema Guild staff, working closely with the producers, analyzes its marketing strengths and weaknesses, determines primary and secondary target audiences, decides on the most appropriate promotional and marketing methods and establishes a sales strategy and release pattern that will guarantee the best possible results in terms of publicity, number of viewers and gross receipts. Promotional flyers are prepared on each film and are used in direct mail campaigns targeted at the company's mailing list as well as acquired lists. Each new release is also entered in important and/or appropriate film and video festivals, or has showings arranged at academic conferences, trade shows and other professional gatherings. Company representatives attend many conferences and markets, with an exhibit booth. The Cinema Guild also arranges press screenings and sends review tapes to appropriate publications, as well as sending out press releases to several hundred periodicals. A full range of advertising and publicity materials are prepared, including posters, leaflets, ad slicks, duplicate photos, and press kits. The Cinema Guild provides regular reports to producers, including copies of published reviews, notification of festival awards and cash prizes, and publicity notices from screenings. Producers' distribution reports are biannual and provide information on name and location of the customer and the nature of the transaction.

Year established: 1975

Area(s) of specialty: Non-theatrical, television and home video distribution

Company officers: Philip Hobel, chairman, Mary-Ann Hobel, chairman, Gary Crowdus, general manager

Number of employees: 5

Contact: Gary Crowdus

CINEPIX FILM PROPERTIES, INC.

900 Broadway, Suite 800
New York, NY 10003
Telephone: (212) 995-9662
Fax: (212) 475-2284

Cinepix Film Properties, Inc., is a thirty-year-old Canadian independent film distribution and production company, which established this New York office in 1995 to accommodate its U.S. distribution and production operations. It is looking for quality features and documentaries, its major avenues of acquisition include the major festivals such as Cannes, Toronto, Montreal and Sundance as well as mid-sized festivals. Plans are to release about 6 films a year, in the $2-4 million range. It is committed to special nurture and marketing of its films for a complete release. It can organize the video and cable release as well as theatrical distribution, and is open to completion financing arrangements or advances. Some of its initial releases are *Fun; Pushing Hands;* and *Lotto Land.*

Year established: 1995

Area(s) of specialty: Fiction feature films

Company officers: Adam Rogers, vice president, U.S. distribution, Amanda Sherwin, director, U.S. distribution

Contact: Amanda Sherwin

CINEQUANON RELEASING CORPORATION

8489 West Third Street
Los Angeles, CA 90048
(213) 658-6043
Fax: (213) 658-6087

Cinequanon is a full service theatrical distribution company. In 1995, it released *Life and Death of the Hollywood Kid.*

Year established: 1994

CINEVISTA, INC.

560 West 43rd Street, Suite 8J
New York, NY 10036
Telephone: (212) 947-4373
Fax: (212) 947-0644

Cinevista, Inc., with over 30 titles in its library, provides special handling for a small number of innovative features, including foreign and English language productions. It distributes to theatrical and television (public, pay, network, cable) markets throughout Canada, Europe and Asia. The company will look at original scripts, and also considers new works from the festival circuit, screenings, and submissions from independent producers. Representatives attend many international festivals, and have participated in such markets as MIPCOM, Monte Carlo, MIP-TV, Berlin, Cannes, IFFM and AFM. It also has a home video line, with its own titles as well as a few titles released by other distributors. Titles in the Cinevista catalog include *Dark Habits; What Have I Done to Deserve This?; Pepi Luci Bom; Law of Desire; Matador; Labyrinth of Passion; Taxi Zum Klo; A Man Like Eva; Cousin Bobby; Caravaggio; In a Glass Cage; Black Lizard; Okoge; Forever Mary; The Everlasting Family; Funny Dirty Little War; The City and the Dogs; Doña Herlinda and Her Son; Time Expired; Zero Patience; Amazing Grace;* and *On My Own.* Cinevista also has put together a Derek Jarman Collection and a Pasolini Collection, as well as a video line, Cinevista Video.

Year established: 1982

Area(s) of specialty: Feature films

Company officers: Rene Fuentes-chao, president

Number of employees: 4

Contact: Rene Fuentes-chao

CLEARVUE

6465 North Avondale
Chicago, IL 60631
Telephone: (312) 775-9433
Fax: (312) 775-9855

Clearvue distributes educational videos/CD-ROMs for the pre-school through high school educational market. The company will consider both production and distribution. Programs should meet specific curriculum needs. Works in its catalog include programs on language arts, science, math, guidance, social studies, music and art, and training tapes for business and industry.

Area(s) of specialty: Educational media

Contact: Mary Watanabe, editorial/production manager

COE FILM ASSOCIATES

65 East 96th Street
New York, NY 10128
Telephone: (212) 831-5355
Fax: (212) 996-6728

Coe Film Associates handles finished films, from two minutes to sixty minutes, for adults and children in the areas of entertainment, science, politics, nature, drama, and comedy, both live and animated. The company distributes exclusively to television (primarily public, pay, and cable), as well as placing programs with home video distributors. It has a selection of 5,000 titles, with about 3,000 currently being circulated, which it distributes for about 600 independent producers, distributors, production companies, media organizations, state agencies and cultural organizations. Distribution is worldwide (the company indicates that its results have been most gratifying in sales to foreign markets), to Western Europe, the Middle East, Eastern Europe, Australia and New Zealand, and Japan. The company has agents in several foreign countries, including United Kingdom, France, Australia, Munich and Japan. More than 2,000 shorts for family viewing are packages; some packages/series include children's half-hour specials, children's hour specials, children's features, Emmy Award-winning young people's specials, children's series, Christmas films, educational, nature, hour specials, hour-plus specials, performing arts stories, AFI special films, sports specials, and other series. All publicity is done in-house, with promotional materials in the form of releases and special flyers; the company also tailors presentations for the requirements of specific customers. Coe prefers finished films, and does not provide advances or guarantees. It works with contract producers and with film schools, markets, and by word-of-mouth to acquire films and videos.

Year established: 1970
Area(s) of specialty: Distribution of films to television
Company officers: Bernice Coe, president, Mignon Levey, sales manager
Number of employees: 8
Contact: Beverly Freeman, acquisitions director

COLUMBIA TRISTAR HOME VIDEO

10202 West Washington Blvd.
Culver City, CA 90232
Telephone: (310) 280-8000
Fax: (310) 280-1724

Columbia TriStar Home Video, the video distribution arm for Sony Pictures Entertainment, releases the films of Columbia Pictures and TriStar Pictures to the worldwide home entertainment market in the videocassette, laserdisc and 8mm formats. With more than 2,500 titles in its library, it is one of the largest manufacturers of home video entertainment in the world. Besides releasing the films from Columbia Pictures and TriStar

Pictures, the Burbank-based video division also distributes to the home video domestic market product for New Line Home Video, MDP Video, IRS Media, Cinetel and various other independent production entities. Internationally, CTHV has a distribution agreement with Turner Entertainment and Castle Rock in selected countries. The company has also begun to distribute a very limited number of video games. In 1991, the Sony Corporation bought out the RCA half of the former joint venture RCA/Columbia Pictures Home Video to form this company. There are offices or representatives in approximately 40 countries around the world.

Year established: 1979

Area(s) of specialty: Pre-recorded tapes, laserdiscs

Company officers: Benjamin Feingold, president, William Chardavoyne, executive vice president, Allan Pritchard, executive vice president, Paul Culbers, executive vice president (North America), Peter Schlessel, senior vice president, business affairs and acquisitions, Kim Lynch, senior vice president, Lon Van Hurwitz, vice president, marketing (North America), Ralph Walin, senior vice president (North America), Jeff Rabinovitz, vice president, sales (North America), John Reina, vice president, sell-through sales (North America), Lexine Wong, vice president, international, Rudy Vila, vice president and regional director, Latin America, Janet Robertson, vice president and regional director, eastern hemisphere licensing, Fritz Friedman, vice president, worldwide publicity. Peter Schlessel, senior vice president-business affairs and acquisitions, Clint Culpepper, director of acquisitions.

CONCEPT MEDIA

2493 DuBridge Avenue
Irvine, CA 92714-5022
Telephone: (714) 660-0727
Fax: (714) 660-0206

Concept Media distributes educational videos and CD-ROMs in nursing, growth and development, substance abuse, counseling, psychiatry, law enforcement, community service, mental health and microbiology. Its catalog contains about 125 titles covering topics concerning addiction/counseling education, basic nursing, communication, gerontological nursing, holistic health, human development, maternal/child, medical/surgical nursing, mental health/psychiatric nursing, pediatric nursing, pharmacology and drug therapy, physical assessment, sociology, and support/patient education. Its CD-ROM courseware includes works on immobilization and microbiology. Many programs are grouped into specific series. Target audiences include healthcare professionals, college students, and nursing students; the company's non-theatrical markets encompass hospitals, nursing schools, colleges and universities.

Year established: 1969

Area(s) of specialty: Health care, science education

Company officers: Ruth Westphal, president

Number of employees: 30

Contact: Lynne Hart, BSN, RNC

CONCORDE/NEW HORIZONS

11600 San Vicente Blvd.
Los Angeles, CA 90025
Telephone: (310) 826-0978

Concorde/New Horizons distributes dramatic feature films, both productions which it has produced and acquired works, many from the festival circuit. The company makes and distributes 24-36 films a year, and picks up 2-3 features, including science fiction, action and films driven by special effects. Some of the titles it has released include *New Crime City; Caged Heat 3; Saturday Night Special; Revenge of the Red Baron; Prisoners;* and *Dinosaur Island.*

Area of specialty: Feature film production and distribution

Company officers: Roger Corman, president and CEO

Year established: 1983

Contact: Bill Bromiley, executive vice president

CORINTH VIDEO

34 Gansevoort Street
New York, NY 10014-1597
Telephone: (800) 221-4720
Fax: (212) 929-0010

Corinth Video specializes in the video release of works related to the performing arts, including opera, dance, vocal, and theatre, as well as classic television and foreign films. New releases in 1996, available on VHS, Beta and laserdisc, included such works as *La Traviata; Tannhäuser; Flying Dutchman; Fiery Angel; Seven Deadly Sins; Lipstick On Your Collar; Pennies from Heaven; The Man From the Pru;* and *Genghis Cohn.*

Area(s) of specialty: Video distribution

Contact: Peter J. Meyer

CORNELL UNIVERSITY AUDIO-VISUAL RESOURCE CENTER

7-8 Business and Technology Park
Ithaca, NY 14850
Telephone: (607) 255-2090
Fax: (607) 255-9946
e-mail: dist_cent@cce.cornell.edu.

Cornell University Audio-Visual Resource Center has around eight hundred films, videos, audiotapes, slide programs and computer programs in its catalogs in subject areas including agriculture, nutrition/health, environment/ecology, plants, safety, child abuse/child development/family life, and home. All of the programs are intended for educational use at the primary though college and adult levels, as well as in business, government and consumer markets, and include topical documentary features and shorts.

Distribution is worldwide, mostly through news media notices, trade journal reviews and Cornell University faculty support. Many of the programs were produced at Cornell University. Acquired titles should be compatible with other holdings already in the collection (faculty reviews titles before acquisition). Some titles are publicized in individual brochures, including *Susceptible to Kindness: Miss Evers' Boys and the Tuskegee Syphilis Study; Environmental Concerns* (including works on recycling and waste disposal, water/soil, and land use and research); *Families in the Balance; Alcohol IQ Network* (software); and *Resources for Parents, Teachers, Caregivers.*

Year established: 1948

Area(s) of specialty: Agriculture and life sciences, human ecology

Company officers: Richard Gray, librarian and director, Elizabeth Powers, assistant librarian, Gerald Kalk, technician

Number of employees: 3

Contact: Richard Gray

CRM FILMS

2215 Faraday Avenue
Carlsbad, CA 92008
Telephone: (619) 431-9800
Fax: (619) 931-5792

CRM Films is a leading producer and provider of corporate training films and related materials. Subjects covered include communication, productivity improvement, empowerment, leadership development, total quality management, team building, staff development and customer satisfaction. Some recent releases include *Meeting Robbers; An Invisible Man Meets the Mummy; Race Without a Finish Line; Team Creativity; Leadership and the New Science; It's a Dog's World; Workteams;* and *The Wizard of Oz.*

Year established: 1988

Area(s) of specialty: Business training and educational film and video

Company officers: Peter J. Jordan, CEO and president

Number of employees: 35

CS ASSOCIATES

52 Simon Willard Road
Concord, MA 01742
Telephone: (508) 287-6100
Fax: (508) 287-6161
e-mail: csa@tiac.net
102 E. Blithedale Avenue
Mill Valley, CA 94941
Telephone: (415) 383-6060
Fax: (415) 383-2520
e-mail: programs@csassociates.com

CS Associates provides two services for the television program producers it represents: distribution of existing programs to broadcasters in the US and abroad, and securing co-production or pre-sale funds from those sources. It is looking for "compelling, well-made programs" on any topic, narrative and documentary films that either fit certain commonly viewed program subject matter (i.e., nature, current affairs magazine format, children's programming, religion) or have broad appeal for the audience of the size required by television here and abroad. Most sales are made to foreign broadcasters, as well as to public and cable television companies in the US. CS Associates has set up a video distribution and fulfillment network, including catalogs and on-air cassette offers from television broadcast, all to increase net income versus using a video distributor. The company attends and takes exhibition space at major foreign television sales markets each year and maintains personal contacts through frequent sales trips, mailings and telephone contacts. Some of the programs and series currently represented are *Frontline; The Civil War; Satya: A Prayer for the Enemy; Children of Fate; Brooklyn Bridge; Eternity; Dark Circle; Scientific American Frontiers; Nanook of the North; Baseball; Castle, Cathedral, Pyramid; Saviors of the Forest; Ishi: The Last Yahi; Bound by the Wind; Pacific Century; The Money Lenders; Road Scholar;* and *The Day After Trinity.*

Year established: 1980

Area(s) of specialty: International television distribution

Number of employees: 2

Contact: Charles Schuerhoff

CURB ENTERTAINMENT INTERNATIONAL CORP.

3907 West Alameda Avenue, Suite 102
Burbank, CA 91505
Telephone: (818) 843-8580
Fax: (818) 566-1719

Curb Entertainment International Corporation was founded to concentrate on worldwide motion picture distribution. It plans individualized marketing strategies for each film and works closely with buyers on an international level. Some of its product includes *The Feminine Touch; Risk; Inside Monkey Zetterland; Lightning in a Bottle; Rave Review; Molly & Gina; The Legend of O.B. Taggart;* and *sex, lies and videotape.*

Year established: 1988

Area(s) of specialty: Distribution of feature fiction films.

Company officers: Carole Curb, president, Brandi Wright, director, international distribution

Contact: Christina Melin, sales and acquisitions

DARINO FILMS

222 Park Avenue South
New York, NY 10003
Telephone: (212) 228-4024
Fax: (212) 228-3767

Darino Films, with over two hundred titles in its library (as well as a six hundred-title classic movies collection), distributes to non-theatrical, television and foreign markets, as well as to home video. The company looks for science and technology material for an ongoing television show, as well as for animation and children's films. Some of its titles include *The Fillers Show; English for Business; Save the Earth; Science 2000; Planet Earth Reports; Our Body-Our Health*. Representatives attend MIP-TV, MIPCOM, Monte Carlo, NATPE, Cannes, and IFFM. It distributes to more than sixty eight countries, in which it maintains a steady clientele in foreign television (the bulk of its distribution). Much of its work is from its own studio, and it accepts submissions which fit within its guidelines, with payment on a percentage basis.

Year established: 1972

Area(s) of specialty: Alternative films, science, television, children

Company officers: Ed Darino

Number of employees: 3

Contact: Ed Darino

DEVILLIER DONEGAN ENTERPRISES

4401 Connecticut Avenue, NW
Washington, DC 20008
Telephone: (202) 686-3980
Fax: (202) 686-3999

Devillier Donegan Enterprises is a program development and distribution company serving independent producers, cable networks and broadcasters throughout the world. It has worked to assist producers and broadcasters with the development of new programming and arranging co-production financing, and has developed and placed series and specials on The Learning Channel, PBS, NHK, ABC, CBS, Channel Four, Cinemax, Comedy Central, National Geographic, A&E, Showtime, BBC, and Premiere Medien GMBH. In 1994 it formed a new company in partnership with Capital Cities/ABC to enable it to take advantage of opportunities in television, cable and satellite technology and expand development, production and distribution efforts internationally. Its program catalog contains the Cap Cities/ABC Non-Fiction Program Catalogue and North American and international animated shorts, children/family, comedy, documentary (adventure/travel, biography, cinema, general, history, music/dance, science/nature) and drama.

Year established: 1980

Area(s) of specialty: International television distribution

Number of employees: 11

Company officers: Ronald J. Devillier, president and CEO, Brian C. Donegan, executive vice president, Joan E. Lanigan, vice president, legal and business affairs, J. John Esteban, vice president, finance and information systems, Linda M. Ekizian, vice president, international sales

Contact: Joan E. Lanigan

DIRECT CINEMA, LTD.

P.O. Box 10003
Santa Monica, CA 90410
Telephone: (310) 396-4774
Fax: (310) 396-3233
e-mail: directcinema@attmail.com

Direct Cinema, with over six hundred films and videos in its collection, distributes many independent productions—features, documentaries, shorts, experimental, educational, arts and performance, animated, television productions, music—and considers its goal to "put the filmmaker first," working with individual filmmakers to maximize the income returned to each film. Its particular emphasis is on documentaries and live-action works. The company has ten salespeople in the U.S. and Canada, who call on many of the key buyers in the country. Direct Cinema distributes exclusively to all markets—theatrical, non-theatrical, semi-theatrical, television, home video, and specialized home video (non-theatrical films which can be sold to the public for home use or specific business use), in the U.S. and English-speaking foreign markets, including Canada, Australia and New Zealand. Subject matter handled includes arts and crafts, business, contemporary concerns, cultural history, dance, family life, art and entertainment, films for young adults and children, films on filmmaking, Native Americans, profiles, the American West, music, and women. Some of the titles in its extensive collection of independent work include *Adam Clayton Powell; Common Threads: Stories From the Quilt; Artists at Work; Dancing for Mr. B; Fine Food Fine Pastries Open 6 to 9; La Ofrenda; Painting the Town: The Illusionistic Murals of Richard Haas; Super Chief: The Life and Legacy of Earl Warren; Tours to Keep; Gullah Tales; My Man Bovanne; Nobody Listened; Tin Toy; Voices From the Attic; Asylum; The Children's Storefront; Cowboy Poets; The Forward: From Immigrants to Americans; Shoeshine; Legacy of the Hollywood Blacklist; D-Day;* and *No Applause Just Throw Money*. Direct Cinema is unique in that it has developed a market for its videos that is exclusively sell-through, with no rentals of its titles to the home video market.

Year established: 1975

Area(s) of specialty: Documentary videos in the educational and home video markets.

Company officers: Mitchell Block, president, Jan Hofferman, director of marketing and promotion, Joan von Hermann, vice president-operations.

Number of employees: 12

Contact: Mitchell Block

DISTANT HORIZON CORPORATION

8282 Sunset Blvd.
Los Angeles, CA 90046
Telephone: (213) 848-4140
Fax: (213) 848-4144

Distant Horizon distributes feature films to theatrical, television and home video markets. Many of its past successes have been works created by first-time writer/directors; it is also looking for work with U.S. box office potential by accomplished directors. The company analyzes scripts and works-in-progress with an eye toward producing those projects; it may fully finance for world rights or supply finishing funds for negotiated rights. With over 30 titles in its collection, it has distributed and/or produced such films as *Chain of Desire*; *Sarafina!*; *Cry the Beloved Country*; *Place of Weeping*; *Scorpion Spring*; and *Captives*. In 1995, three of its features were in theatrical release.

Year established: 1986

Area(s) of specialty: Independent features for theatrical release

Company officers: Anant Singh, Paul Janssen, Brian Cox

Number of employees: 10

Contact: Jennifer Ivory

DMS EXPORT IMPORT

1540 North Highland, Ste. 110
Hollywood, CA 90028
Telephone: (213) 466-0121
Fax: (213) 466-0515

This company distributes feature films, documentaries, and live sports shows. It is looking for productions to sell to Eastern European and Far Eastern countries. Its primary markets are non-theatrical and home video, as well as all television.

Year established: 1979

Area(s) of specialty: Feature films

Company officers: Mariusz Sosnowski, Larry Fine

Number of employees: 4

Contact: Larry S. Fine

DREAM ENTERTAINMENT

8489 West 3rd Street, Suite 1096
Los Angeles, CA 90048
Telephone: (213) 655-5501
Fax: (213) 655-5603

Dream Entertainment specializes in the production and distribution of quality films with budgets up to $2,000,000, and is interested in developing long-term relationships with independent filmmakers.

Year established: 1992

Area(s) of specialty: Fiction features

Company officers: Ehud Bleiberg, CEO

Contact: Lynn Mooney, vice president, sales/acquisitions

DRIFT RELEASING

611 Broadway, Suite 742
New York, NY 10012
Telephone: (212) 254-4118
Fax: (212) 254-3154

Drift Releasing handles documentaries and dramatic films that are generally considered to be less commercial "quality" art films; it also handles foreign films, films by first-time directors, and "more challenging films in terms of narrative and theme." It seeks out films that "attract film-literate audiences," so distribution strategies focus on larger cities and college towns. There are currently sixteen films in its collection, all in active distribution. Some titles are *Germany Year 90 Nine Zero; Profession Neo Nazi; Fast Trip, Long Drop; The Darker Side of Black*; and *My Crasy Life*. Drift will offer advance/guarantees on primarily exclusive rights in North America. Festivals offer the primary road to acquisitions.

Year established: 1994

Area(s) of specialty: European and American drama and documentary

Company officers: Chris Hoover, Toby Vann, David Barker, Brian Goldberg

Number of employees: 5

Contact: Chris Hoover

EDUCATIONAL PRODUCTIONS, INC.

7412 SW Beaverton Hillsdale Highway, Suite 210
Portland, OR 97725
Telephone: (503) 292-9234/(800) 950-4949
Fax: (503) 292-9246

Educational Productions specializes in programs that help adults learn to work with typically developing and special needs young children. Its markets include school districts, colleges and universities, Head Start programs, hospitals, clinics and daycare programs; professionals who work with children from birth to eight years as well as parents. All programs are produced in series; there are currently six series with a total of 27 programs. It includes *First Steps: Supporting Early Language Development; Good Talking With You: Language Acquisition Through Conversation;* and *Play Power: Skill Building for Young Children.* The company acquires only fully completed programs, with quality and instructional design being chief concerns.

Year established: 1982

Area(s) of specialty: Training professionals and parents in early childhood education, early childhood special education

Company officers: Linda Freedman, president, Rae Latham, vice president

Number of employees: 11

Contact: Linda Freedman

EDUCATIONAL VIDEO CENTER

352 Park Avenue South, 4th Floor
New York, NY 10010
Telephone: (212) 725-3534
Fax: (212) 725-6501

Educational Video Center is a non-profit media center "dedicated to empowering inner city youth through the creative use of media." It distributes its own titles, video documentaries produced by high school students or its YO-TV program for high school graduates. The tapes are "powerful expressions of the problems young people face every day at home, in school, and on the streets of their communities." Its productions have won over 60 awards nationally and internationally and have broadcast on cable and network television. There are over 50 titles in its collection; some recent titles are *Guns and the Lives They Leave Holes In; State of Emergency* (on budget cuts in NYC); and *School of Many Colors* (on multicultural education). Programs are distributed to schools, teachers, community based organizations, universities and libraries.

Year established: 1984

Area(s) of specialty: Youth-produced documentary video

Company officers: Alan Dichter, chairman of board, Steven Goodman, executive director, Zoya Kocur, associate director

Number of employees: 5 full-time, 7 part-time

Contact: Zoya Kocur

THE EDUCATIONAL VIDEO GROUP

242 Southwind Way
Greenwood, IN 46142
Telephone: (317) 888-6581
Fax: (317) 881-5857
e-mail: 75047.620@compuserve.com

The Educational Video Group handles documentary and educational productions—history, speech and communications, health, sports, theater, broadcast, and public relations. Distribution is worldwide. Currently, it has sixty one titles in its library, all of which are actively distributed, and it also works with contract producers. Clients include libraries, colleges and secondary schools.

Year established: 1985

Area(s) of specialty: Education, speech communication

Company officers: Roger Cook, president

Number of employees: 10

Contact: Thomas Stumph, Beth Haynes

ELECTRONIC ARTS INTERMIX

536 Broadway, 9th Floor
New York, NY 10012
Telephone: (212) 966-4605
Fax: (212) 941-6118

Electronic Arts Intermix (EAI) is a nonprofit media arts center which is a major international resource for independent video. EAI "supports the alternative voices and personal visions of independent videomakers within the context of contemporary art media and culture," as well as providing services to artists and audiences throughout the country and internationally. Its Artists' Videotape Distribution Service is "one of the world's pre-eminent distributors of artists' videotapes." The collection provides a major source of programming for educational, cultural and art institutions, as well as television, and represents a broad survey of international media art production from the 1960s to the 1990s. There are over 1,850 tapes by more than 155 artists from the U.S., Europe, Australia, Latin America and Japan. EAI publishes a comprehensive catalog, along with a supplement and update information, which contains biographical and contextual information on artists, descriptions of tapes, artists' videographies and an international bibliography. Tapes are distributed to international and regional museums, art centers, galleries, universities, and libraries, as well as cable, broadcast and satellite systems. EAI's related activities are educational and curatorial services, programming consultations, materials and a tape archive. Its Preservation Program allows many historically significant works to be available through the distribution service.

Year established: 1971

Area(s) of specialty: Video by artists

Company officers: Lori Zippay, executive director, Stephen Vitiello, distribution director, Robert Beck, technical director, David Kalal, D/A assistant

Number of employees: 5

Contact: Stephen Vitiello

ENTERTAINMENT STUDIOS, INC.

9830 Mohrs Cove Lane
Windermere, FL 34786
Telephone: (407) 291-8965
Fax: (407) 291-8988

This company distributes feature films. There are currently 14 in its library, with 3 in active distribution, including such titles as *Even Angels Fall; Fatal Passion; Rookie Vampire;* and *Caribbean Ghost.*

Year established: 1993

Area(s) of specialty: Motion picture production and distribution

Contact: Hugh Parks

ENVIRONMENTAL MEDIA CORPORATION

P.O. Box 1016
Chapel Hill, NC 27514
Telephone: (919) 933-3003
Fax: (919) 942-8785

Environmental Media Corporation produces and distributes media that supports environmental education. The company distributes to broadcast, cable, satellite and non-broadcast markets.

Area(s) of specialty: Environmental media

Company officers: Bill Pendergraft, Gwen Gerber

Contact: Bill Pendergraft

ETR ASSOCIATES

P.O. Box 1830
Santa Cruz, CA 95061
Telephone: (408) 438-4080 x238
Fax: (408) 438-4284

This company distributes health education videos and materials geared to K-12, clinics, and health care providers. Subject areas covered in its catalog include violence/injury prevention, HIV/AIDS/STD, sexuality, reproductive health, maternal and child health, tobacco/drugs.

Area(s) of specialty: Health education media

Contact: John Thompson, acquisitions editor

EXPANDED ENTERTAINMENT

28024 Dorothy Drive
Agoura Hills, CA 91301
Telephone: (818) 991-2884
Fax: (818) 991-3773

Expanded Entertainment specializes in animation programs, distributing to theatrical, non-theatrical, home video and television markets. It "represents the highest quality in animation in the world"; it looks at quality, story development and character development. The company is also now the executive producer of an upcoming television series. It has more than five hundred titles in its collection, including such films as *Creature Comforts; Balance; Technological Threat;* and *The Great Cognito.* Company representatives attend animation festivals such as Annecy, Hiroshima, and Ottawa to look for acquisitions, and it also looks at submissions from producers.

Year established: 1984

Area(s) of specialty: Animation

Company officers: Terry Thoren, president, Bill Buck, general manager

Number of employees: 7

Contact: Bill Buck

FACETS MULTIMEDIA, INC.

1517 West Fullerton Avenue
Chicago, IL 60614
Telephone: (312) 281-9075
Fax: (312) 929-5437
e-mail: milos@facets.org

Facets Video is a home video distributor of over 26,000 foreign, independent classic American, silent, documentary, experimental, fine art, classical music, jazz and blues, and quality children's videos and laser discs to the home video market. Emphasis is on the art of cinema, with the bulk of the collection being features and documentaries. Of the titles Facets distributes, the majority are handled on a non-exclusive basis, with about 160 titles licensed exclusively for the U.S. and Canadian home video markets. It publishes several catalogs, including a 300-page major catalog and specialized catalogs such as African-American films and New Visions, a catalog of international and independent film and video artists. The films on tape are available for rental by mail throughout the continental U.S. Facets acquires tapes "not because they generated $100 million at the box office or because they have 'star value,' but because the maker of the film or video has something to say and a challenging, new way in which to say it." It adds hundreds of tapes to its collection each month.

Year founded: 1975

Area(s) of specialty: Independent features, documentaries, foreign films

Company officers: Milos Stehlik, director, Nicole Dreiske, artistic director, Catherine Foley, marketing manager

Number of employees: 46

Contact: Milos Stehlik

FANLIGHT PRODUCTIONS

47 Halifax Street
Boston, MA 02130
Telephone: (617) 937-4113
Fax: (617) 524-8838

Fanlight Productions distributes films and videos on society and the human condition, with a special focus on issues relating to health care, mental health and psychology, disabilities, aging, family and sex roles, the workplace, and professional ethics. It does not primarily look for straightforward training programs, but rather films which "convey a sense of involvement and immediacy, and which will have the kind of intellectual and emotional impact on audiences which stimulates discussion and motivates changes in behavior." Most of its clients strongly prefer films which are thirty minutes or less, though it considers longer productions as well. The majority of releases are documentaries, and it will also consider dramatic, animated and experimental productions. Fanlight's primary distribution efforts focus on the non-theatrical, educational market, and it has a strong customer base in universities (including schools of nursing, medicine and allied health), hospitals and other health care organizations; community health, mental health and disability groups, government agencies, public and professional libraries, and similar institutions. Most of its more than 130 titles are aimed at audiences at the junior college level and up (including professionals), although it is expanding its collection of programming for high school audiences. It also handles television and cable sales, and international marketing, particularly in English-speaking countries. Some recent acquisitions include *When Billy Broke His Head; When the Brain Goes Wrong; Something Should be Done About Grandma Ruthie;* and *Code Gray.* Its catalogs are mailed twice annually, and three times a year it also publishes a newsletter focusing on its new releases. Flyers on groups of

films in a particular subject area are created and mailed whenever appropriate; telemarketing efforts are generally targeted at determining the best audiences and marketing strategies for handling new releases. The company welcomes the opportunity to look at proposals, scripts and especially rough cuts of films in its areas of interest, and is frequently able to make suggestions which will increase the marketability of a production. It can also provide letters of interest and support for funding proposals of projects which appear promising. It generally offers standard royalty arrangements, based on a percentage of gross receipts. It does not make guarantees and is rarely in a position to offer significant advances, although it will sometimes do so in the case of an especially promising project. The great majority of Fanlight's releases are by independent producers. It looks for new productions at festivals and conferences, film schools, word-of-mouth, advertising in publications such as *The Independent* and *International Documentary*, and through constant monitoring of the journals and other publications in each of its areas of interest. It also acquires a number of programs each year at the film market of the National Educational Media Network. Fanlight also frequently takes on films by young, unknown, student or first-time producers, and also handles programs on difficult and controversial topics.

Year established: 1980

Area(s) of specialty: Health, mental health, disabilities, gerontology, family, workplace

Company officers: Ben Achtenberg, president, Karen McMillen, marketing director

Number of employees: 4-5

Contact: Karen McMillen, Amy Brisebois

FILM IDEAS, INC.

3710 Commercial Avenue, Suite 13
Northbrook, IL 60062
Telephone: (800) 475-3456
Fax: (708) 480-7496

Film Ideas, Inc., handles documentary and educational works. It looks for "unique approaches and hard-to-find topics" and evaluates each production for its unique potential. With about 500 titles in its library, it distributes works which deal with violence and conflict, mathematics, science, history, and social studies. The titles in its library are aimed at students, the general population and health care professionals in the non-theatrical market, with some television distribution. Film Ideas will pay advances, and contracts are also based on royalty agreements. The company will look at works-in-progress.

Year established: 1979

Area(s) of specialty: Education, health care

Company officers: Michael Collins, Alice Collins

Number of employees: 15

Contact: Alice Collins

FILMHAUS

2255 West Sepulveda Blvd., Suite 204
Torrance, CA 90501
Telephone: (310) 320-8383
Fax: (310) 320-8384

This newly formed distribution company caters to the arthouse circuit with low-budget independent American fiction films. Some of its releases are *Mod Fuck Explosion; Liability Crisis; Two Plus One; City Unplugged; The Bed You Sleep In;* and *Restless Garden.* The company initially plans small limited releases, with 1-2 prints per release, moving up to 5-10 prints.

Year established: 1994

Area(s) of specialty: Art house releases

Company officers: Gregory Hatanaka

Contact: Gregory Hatanaka

FILM-MAKERS' COOPERATIVE

175 Lexington Avenue
New York, NY 10016
Telephone: (212) 889-3820

Film-Makers' Cooperative was created by artists "as a multi-faceted organization for the promotion of alternative film culture" and today boasts one of the largest collections of independent and avant-garde films and videos in the world. Over 3,000 titles are in the catalog, which is often used as a basic reference work for historians and critics; over 650 filmmakers are listed, and annual supplements are issued. Use of the Film-Makers' Cooperative is open to any filmmaker who wishes to deposit a print; prices are set by the makers, who also provide the descriptions. The company is nonprofit, nondiscriminating and noncontractual; relationships are not exclusive. Operating costs are offset by a percentage of rentals collected; renters cover all shipping and handling charges. All films are handled equally, with no work singled out for individual publicity.

Area of specialty: Independent/avant-garde films

Number of employees: 2

Year established: 1962

Contact: M.M. Serra

FILMMAKERS LIBRARY

124 East 40th Street
New York, NY 10016
Telephone: (212) 808-4980
Fax: (212) 808-4983

Filmmakers Library looks for documentaries, preferably between 30-60 minutes in length, that "are provocative, informative, and have good production qualities." It is especially interested in the areas of women's issues, multicultural issues, psychology, anthropology and international concerns. In addition to these areas of specialization, its collection includes works by many independent filmmakers on the humanities, culture and society, Black studies, history, behavioral science, aging, health, nature, science and ecology. There are a total of 500 titles in its library, with 400 in active distribution. Among these titles are *It Was A Wonderful Life; Total Baby; In Search of Our Fathers; Fire Eyes; Human Tide; El Salvador: Talking to the Enemy; Wild Swans; High School of American Dreams; Not Without My Veil; Between Black and White; Chelyabinsk; Beautiful Piggies; Sex Games; Kasthuri; Tears Are Not Enough; Musical Steppes of Mongolia; Mountains of Gold; Drug Mules; Methadone—Curse or Cure?; Rajneeshpuram; Survivors; Until the Cure, I Offer the Care; Not a Simple Story/Out in Silence; Another First Step; When Women Kill;* and *Breakdown*. Filmmakers Library produces brochures, study guides, targeted postcard mailings, involves special interest groups in the area of the film's subject, attends markets and conferences (MIP, IFFM, and Berlin in alternate years), has films reviewed in publications, and enters films in festivals. It also utilizes telephone marketing. Distribution is nationwide, as well as to Canada and Australia. Primary clients include universities, public libraries, community groups, high schools and hospitals.

Year established: 1969

Area(s) of specialty: Non-theatrical distribution

Company officers: Sue E. Oscar, Linda Gottesman

Number of employees: 3

Contact: Sue E. Oscar, Linda Gottesman

FILMOPOLIS PICTURES

11300 W. Olympic Blvd., Suite 840
Los Angeles, CA 90064
Telephone: (310) 914-1776
Fax: (310) 914-1777

Filmopolis Pictures' goal is "to bring the most innovative and stimulating films from around the world to American audiences", including works "from the most independent of filmmakers to firmly established masters." The company is an independent motion picture company formed by a merger between India-based production company C.E.G. Worldwide and North American theatrical distributor FilmHaus Releasing. It plans to distribute 8-10 films annually in all media, releasing each title in the major metropolitan markets followed by release to home video and television. In addition to distribution, Filmopolis also plans to produce at least 2-3 films annually. It currently has 25 titles in its library; some of its releases include *Talk; Traps; Ma Saison Preferée (My Favorite Season)*; and *Target*. The company will consider completion financing, advances, minimum guarantee, negative pickups.

Year established: 1995
Area(s) of specialty: Theatrical, home video, domestic television
Company officers: Zachary Lovas, Jason Lovas, Ray Kavandi
Number of employees: 7
Contact: David Klein

FILMS AROUND THE WORLD/FILMWORLD TELEVISION, INC.

342 Madison Avenue, Suite 812
New York, NY 10173
Telephone: (212) 599-9500
Fax: (212) 599-6040
e-mail: alexjr@pipeline.com

Films Around the World, Inc., is a New York corporation founded in 1930 by film agent/distributor Irvin Shapiro. Its affiliated company, Filmworld Television, Inc., specializes in television sales. The two companies, and a number of other affiliates, own, co-own, represent as sales agent, and distribute a library of approximately 500 feature films, plus a number of television series, shorts, and documentaries. The company has represented documentaries, but prefers to handle series only. Its primary goal is licensing to distributors, but it does distribute directly to video and television itself. The company actively seeks out programming to fill a buyer's specific requirement. Sales are made primarily from the New York offices. One affiliate produced or co-produced more than a dozen features during 1988/89. One company represents an Italian distributor/investor which has been seeking co-production opportunities; Films Around the World is actively looking for projects which meet their requirements—MOW or cable domestic presale, domestic theatrical distribution agreement coupled with 50% of financing—so that foreign distributors can consider financing, in whole or part, the production. Another affiliate, Showcase Productions, Inc., owns or co-owns a large library of the best known prime time dramatic programming from the '50s.

Year established: 1930
Area(s) of specialty: Domestic and international sales/licensing of independent features, television series, MOWs
Company officers: Alexander W. Kogan, Jr., Beverly Partridge, Deborah Dave
Number of employees: 7
Contact: Alexander W. Kogan, Jr.,

FILMS FOR EDUCATORS, INC./FILMS FOR TELEVISION

420 East 55th Street, Suite 6U
New York, NY 10022
Telephone: (212) 486-6577
Fax: (212) 980-9826

This company was formed as a woman-owned business specializing in sales and rentals of educational and documentary films to schools and libraries. In the 80's it formed its Environmental Awareness Series, a compilation of high-tech scientific environmental videos that address multi-dimensional needs of communities and cities, and the company is now involved in worldwide distribution of environmental programming. Some of the topics carried in this series include air pollution, endangered species, environmental awareness, environmental biology, environmental disaster, environmental law, horses and the handicapped, land reclamation, noise pollution, pesticide training, radiation, recycling, solid waste management, toxic waste, transportation alternatives, volcanoes, water conservation, wildlife, and topography, climate and vegetation.

Year established: 1976

Contact: Distribution coordinator

FILMS FOR THE HUMANITIES AND SCIENCES, INC.®

P.O. Box 2053
Princeton, NJ 08543-2053
Telephone: (800) 257-5126/(609) 275-1400
Fax: (609) 275-3767

Films for the Humanities and Sciences® (FFHS) is one of the largest distributors of educational audiovisual materials to schools, colleges, libraries, hospitals, and businesses. With over 5,500 titles in its library, FFHS provides a comprehensive selection of video, videodisc, and CD-ROM titles in a wide variety of subject areas, including the arts, literature, foreign languages, humanities, social studies, science, health, psychology, business, and communications. FFHS has received numerous industry awards and citations for the quality of its programs. Recent releases include *English Poetry Plus* on CD-ROM; *Jane Austen and Her World; Journal of the First Americans; Discovering Women: Six Remarkable Women Scientists; People in Motion: Changing Ideas About Physical Disability; What Can We Do About Violence?; Journey to the Centers of the Brain; Basic Laboratory Chemistry; Physics in Action;* and 500 additional new titles.

Year established: 1971

Area(s) of specialty: Educational video, videodisc, CD-ROM

Company officers: Harold Mantell

Number of employees: 45

Contact: Howard Mantell

FIRST LOOK PICTURES RELEASING

8800 Sunset Blvd., #302
Los Angeles, CA 90069
Telephone: (310) 855-1199
Fax: (310) 855-0719

First Look Pictures is a division of Overseas Film Group. It assists producers in the packaging and financing of a range of projects, including specialty films and genre releases. Selected arthouse features are also domestically distributed. Some of its releases include *The Secret of Roan Inish; The Scent of Green Papaya; Party Girl;* and *Antonia's Passion.*
Area(s) of specialty: Fiction features
Company officers: Ellen Little, president, Robert Little, chairman, Maud Nadler, director, creative affairs, M.J. Peckos, senior vice president, distribution and marketing
Contact: M.J. Peckos

FIRST RUN FEATURES AND FIRST RUN/ICARUS

153 Waverly Place, 6th Floor
New York, NY 10014
Telephone: (212) 243-0600/(800) 876-1710
Fax: (212) 989-7649

First Run Features is one of three closely affiliated companies, including First Run/Icarus Films and Icarus International. First Run Features distributes American and foreign independent features, home video and television, while First Run/Icarus deals almost exclusively with non-theatrical and semi-theatrical markets and Icarus handles foreign markets, particularly television in Europe. Recent releases include *Paul Bowles: The Complete Outsider; The Life and Times of Alan Ginsberg; Living Proof: HIV and the Pursuit of Happiness; Sunday's Children; The Sex of the Stars; Midnight Dancers; Heaven's a Drag;* and *Blush.* Home video is a large part of First Run's business. The company specializes in Swedish, religious and alternative lifestyle films. It has 90 titles in its library, with approximately 20 new releases each year. Representatives attend Toronto, Berlin, IFFM and other festivals and markets. First Run/Icarus has a library of over 300 films, and averages about 40 new releases each year. The collection is particularly strong on independent productions on Latin America, South Africa, the Middle East, women's issues, gay and lesbian issues, civil rights and labor; some of the other categories it handles are animation, art/photography, cinema studies, economics, religion, environment, ecology, and education. That library includes such works as *Sherman's March; 28 Up; Dance of Hope; Promises to Keep; Bombs Aren't Cool!; She Must Be Seeing Things; Weapons of the Spirit;* and *Cane Toads.* Target audiences include public libraries, college and university faculty and libraries, student film societies and activist groups, public schools identified through customer lists, purchased lists, associations, festivals and markets.
Area(s) of specialty: Independent films, documentary films
Company officers: Seymour Wishman
Contact: Marc Mauceri

FLOWER FILMS AND VIDEO

10341 San Pablo Avenue
El Cerrito, CA
Telephone: (510) 525-0942

Flower Films is the company of independent filmmaker Les Blank and was founded to distribute numerous films on "spirited people, music, food and other passions" produced by his company, including such works as *Burden of Dreams; Gap-Toothed Women; Always for Pleasure; Cigarette Blues; Garlic is as Good as Ten Mothers; The Blues According to Lightnin' Hopkins;* and *In Heaven There Is No Beer?*. Flower also distributes other works by independent filmmakers, including such works as *Chopi Music of Mozambique; Clifton Chenier, the King of Zydeco; Dancing Outlaw; Music of the Spirits; Perfumed Nightmare; Photo Album; Talking Feet; Tree of Life; Turumba; Zydeco;* and *'N' is a Number*. Works are distributed both theatrically and non-theatrically, as well as on home video.

Year established: 1967

Area(s) of specialty: Cultural documentaries

Contact: Les Blank

FOX LORBER ASSOCIATES, INC.

419 Park Avenue South, 20th Floor
New York, NY 10016
Telephone: (212) 686-6777
Fax: (212) 685-2625

Founded in 1981, Fox Lorber Associates, Inc., distributes film, television and video properties in all markets worldwide, with the main thrust of its business focused on international film and television programming sales, domestic home video distribution, and domestic television sales. Launched in 1990, Fox Lorber Home Video, distributed by Orion, has a large market share for the distribution of critically acclaimed foreign language features, American independent and classic art films. The company distributes over 500 individual titles and series representing over 1,000 hours of programming from a diverse group of suppliers. Its buyers represent all major television, cable and satellite networks, and film and video companies domestically and abroad. Fox Lorber seeks to acquire "quality programming which meets market needs—domestically and internationally." International distribution activities include worldwide representation of dramas, documentaries, and family series from the South African Broadcasting Corporation, the output of French Public Television for distribution in the U.S, and Tilt 23 1/2, a series produced by Fujisankei of Japan. It has also handled major feature film libraries including Atlantic Entertainment, Kings Road Entertainment, documentary collections such those of Time/Life Films, and Kodak Video Trips travel library. The company recently acquired worldwide distribution rights to the AIMS Media library, with over 1,000 programs. In the U.S., Fox Lorber licenses programming to all the major cable networks and public television outlets, including HBO, Discovery Channel, Arts and Entertainment, Encore, The Disney Channel and Showtime. It was one of the first companies to negotiate a package of features for the Sundance Film Channel. Representatives participate in all major markets and festivals, including MIPCOM, NATPE, MIP-TV, Cannes, Los Angeles Screenings, DISCOP-EAST, VSDA, London Program Market, and MIP ASIA. Fox Lorber Home Video has a library of over 100 titles, including *Closely Watched Trains; The Official Story; Pathfinder; Children of Nature; Memories of a Marriage; The Icicle Thief; The Trial; The Killer; Hard-Boiled; The Vanishing; A Taxing Woman; Doña Flor and Her Two Husbands; 28 Up;* and *Brother's Keeper.* Two newly launched specialty labels are Forum Home Video, which released the *Joan Collins Personal Workout;* and *Mondo Pop,* a collaboration with Streamline Pictures which specializes in live-action cutting-edge science fiction and fantasy films. It has also been involved in alternative home video distribution activities, helping to establish a home video label for the Arts and Entertainment Network that pioneered specialty off-air catalog sales direct to consumer and a partnership with Ingram Entertainment to establish Monarch Home Video, a house brand label for independent films.

Year established: 1980

Area(s) of specialty: Foreign sales, domestic home video

Company officers: Richard Lorber, CEO, Sheri Levine, executive vice president, international, Michael Olivieri, executive vice president, home video.

Number of employees: 30

Contact: Krysanne Katsoolis, vice president, acquisitions and business affairs, Chris Peeler

FOX SEARCHLIGHT PICTURES

10201 West Pico Blvd.
Building 38, Room 110
Los Angeles, CA 90035
Telephone: (310) 369-2011
Fax: (310) 369-2359

Founded in late 1994, Fox Searchlight Pictures is dedicated to the production, acquisition, marketing, and distribution of "sophisticated intelligent" feature films. The company's aim is to release 6-8 films annually, in the $5-15 million budget range, that appeal to the specialized upmarket audience and also have the potential to commercial success. Some of the films it has released include *The Brothers McMullen; Girl 6;* and *The Secret Agent;* future films include *Nocturne; Ice Storm; Flight of the Raven; Good Scent on a Strange Mountain; Wings of an Angel; A Loving Gentleman* and *Boo.* The company is one of four production arms within Fox Filmed Entertainment.

Area(s) of specialty: Fiction features

Contact: Claudia Lewis, vice president production

FRAMELINE DISTRIBUTION
346 Ninth Street
San Francisco, CA 94103
Telephone: (415) 703-8654
Fax: (415) 861-1404
e-mail: frameline@aol.com

Frameline, a non-profit organization, is the only national distributor solely dedicated to the promotion, distribution and exhibition of lesbian and gay films and videotapes. It was established in conjunction with the San Francisco International Lesbian and Gay film Festival. There are over 160 titles in its catalog, encompassing a variety of genres and including features, special programs, animation, documentary, experimental, and shorts on such subjects as activism, aging, AIDS/health, art, music and letters, Asian images, Black images, censorship, coming out, disability, discrimination, drag/transgender/camp, family values, Gay 101, history/herstory, homophobia, Jewish images, Latino/a images, media studies, Native American images, personal expressions, racism, relationships, religion, sexuality, sociology, violence, and youth. The catalog states that Frameline's collection "has expanded to further represent the variety, excellence, innovation and importance of lesbian and gay film and videomaking...(and) the expansion of vision by our makers: the attempt to reflect viewpoints beyond one-dimensional representations of lesbian, gay and bisexual culture." Works are made available on 35mm, 16mm, and video; Frameline is looking for media from communities within the lesbian and gay community (sub-communities). Frameline deals are 40/60 producer/distributor, exclusive, advance print costs; completion money may be available for exceptional cases. Distribution is theatrical, non-theatrical, semi-theatrical and home video. Frameline focuses on community-based work, so it caters to a lot of local film festivals around the U.S. and abroad, and also seeks to better tailor its collection for schools and public libraries. Having the festival attached to the organization does much for the visibility of its distribution program, and is also a source of acquisitions. Some recent releases include *Dyke Drama* (a compilation of four short lesbian stories); *Bête Noire*; *Changing Our Minds: The Story of Dr. Evelyn Hooker*; *Ferdous (Paradise)*; *Joe-Joe*; *Le Ravissement*; *Long Eyes of Earth*; *The Love Thang Trilogy*; *Nitrate Kisses*; *No Porque Fidel Lo Digas (Not Because Fidel Says So)*; *Parole*; *Dangerous When Wet*; *& Stick Figures*; *The Potluck and the Passion*; *Queer Son*; *Thick Lips, Thin Lips*; *Tomboy*; *You Can Open Your Eyes Now*.

Year established: 1980

Area(s) of specialty: Lesbian and gay independent media

Company officers: Tess Martin, executive director, Desi del Valle, distribution associate

Number of employees: 4 full-time/2 part-time

Contact: Desi del Valle

FRIES DISTRIBUTION COMPANY

6922 Hollywood Blvd.
Los Angeles, CA 90028
Telephone: (213) 466-2266

Fries Distribution Comany is a production and distribution company handling features and full length documentaries. It focuses on action/ adventure, drama, comedy, and musicals. Among its titles are *The Burning Bed; Mission of the Shark; Small Sacrifices; Terror at London Bridge; Calendar Girl Murders*; and *Spider-Man Film/Series Package*.

Company officers: Chuck W. Fries, CEO and president

Year established: 1974

Area of specialty: Features and home video.

GLENN PHOTO SUPPLY/GLENN VIDEO VISTAS, LTD.

6924 Canby Avenue, Suite 103
Reseda, CA 91355
Telephone: (818) 881-8110
Fax: (818) 981-5506

This company has a catalog which features over 1,700 films and videos, including features (silent, sound and foreign), documentaries, comedy and dramatic shorts, animation, westerns, sports, musicals, fantasy, women's, trailers, screen tests and out-takes, foreign, experimental and avant-garde works. Primary audiences include educational institutions, museums, and film societies.

Year established: 1959

Area(s) of specialty: Educational and entertainment films

Company officers: Murray Glass, owner-manager

Number of employees: 3

Contact: Murray Glass

SAMUEL GOLDWYN COMPANY

10203 Santa Monica Blvd.
Los Angeles, CA 90067
Telephone: (310) 552-2255
Fax: (310) 284-8493

The Samuel Goldwyn Company is a major independent feature film and television production company. It has released such films as *Much Ado About Nothing; The Wedding Banquet; Eat Drink Man Woman; The Perez Family; Oleanna*; and *Doom Generation*, as well as producing several mass-market television programs. The company has been known for discovering and nurturing talent and filmmakers. It has a video output deal with Hallmark Entertainment, Inc, a unit of Hallmark cards.

Year established: 1979

Area(s) of specialty: Feature film and television production and distribution

Contact: Ronna Wallace, senior vice president, acquisitions

GPN/UNIVERSITY OF NEBRASKA

P.O. Box 80669
Lincoln, NE 68501-0669
Telephone: (800) 228-4630
Fax: (402) 472-4076
e-mail: gpn@unl.edu

GPN is a national and international distributor of educational media, video, videodisc, CD-ROM, and other technologies to the K-12 and higher educational markets. GPN mails over 3,000,000 pieces of direct mail each year. Some examples of titles in its collection include *Reading Rainbow*; *3-2-1 Classroom Contact*; *Ghostwriter*; and *Newton's Apple Mathvantage* for the K-12 market segment. For the post secondary market, GPN distributes *Worlds of Childhood*; *The Chinese*; and many other titles. The company pays royalties based on actual sales; for the right product it will give advances. It is looking for programming appropriate for the in-school market. Producers should submit masters on Beta or 1", color publicity photos, and guide material to accompany the video.

Year established: 1962

Number of employees: 29

Company officers: Lee Rockwell, director, Stephen C. Lenzen, associate director

Area of specialty: Educational video for K-12 and post-secondary

Contact: Gaylen Whited

GRAMERCY PICTURES

9247 Alden Drive
Beverly Hills, CA 90210-3730
Telephone: (310) 777-1960

Gramercy Pictures is a joint venture of MCA Universal and PolyGram. It has released such films as *Four Weddings and a Funeral*; *D.R.O.P. Squad*; *Backbeat*; *Romeo is Bleeding*; *Jason's Lyric*; and *Priscilla, Queen of the Desert*, as well as several lower- to medium-budget pictures. It releases about 15 films each year. 1995 releases include *The Usual Suspects*; *Jack and Sarah*; *Mallrats*; *I'm Not Rappaport*; *Canadian Bacon*; *Carrington*; *Portrait of a Lady*; and *Moonlight and Valentino*.

Number of employees: 45

Company officers: Russell Schwartz, president

Area of specialty: Theatrical motion pictures

GREYCAT FILMS

3829 Delaware Lane
Las Vegas, NV 89109
Telephone: (702) 737-0670
Fax: (702) 737-0670
e-mail: greycat@aol.com

Greycat Films handles feature-length American independent fiction films and documentaries, selected international feature films and documentaries, and occasional short subjects. It specializes in films which are considered risky, "unique, aggressive films" which "push conventional boundaries." Each film is distributed and marketed theatrically according to its own release plan, generally to an audience which is a combination of young intellectuals (18-26), film buffs, and other intellectually active adults. Acquisition is accomplished through direct contact with producers and representatives as well as at selected markets and festivals (such as Seattle, San Francisco, Boston, Toronto, Palm Springs, and the Hamptons). The company also actively pursues distribution "partnerships" with producers. Greycat will look at works-in-progress, but does not actively invest in film production. Its most important market is the theatrical market, which creates the awareness for its ancillary markets; it is just beginning to expand into the non-theatrical market. Some of the films which it has handled include *Henry: Portrait of a Serial Killer* (the company created an "art market" hit for this film, which was produced as direct-to-video), and *1000 Pieces of Gold* (achieved fair theatrical success for this film produced for PBS by targeting selected female patrons). There are about 20 titles in its library, with about 6 being actively distributed; some titles include *Fun; Meet the Feebles* (New Zealand); *Dingo* (Australia); *The Plutonium Circus; The Neapolitan Mathematician* (Italy); *Resident Alien; Singapore Sling* (Greece).

Year established: 1989

Area(s) of specialty: Theatrical distribution, American independent films, foreign films, specialty films

Company officers: Suzanne Bowers Whitten, co-president, David Whitten, co-president

Number of employees: 4

Company officers: Suzanne Whitten

GUIDANCE ASSOCIATES

90 South Bedford Road
Mt. Kisco, NY 10549
Telephone: (914) 666-4100
Fax: (914) 666-0172

Guidance Associates distributes documentaries, narratives and instructional videos. Its Media Center Satellite Network is a distribution system that uses new technology to deliver current educational videos directly to media centers.

Area(s) of specialty: Educational media
Contact: Will Goodman, Willie Mann

HEMDALE ENTERTAINMENT

7966 Beverly Blvd.
Los Angeles, CA 90048-4512
Telephone: (213) 966-3700
Fax: (213) 966-3750

Hemdale is a theatrical film distribution company. Some recent releases include *Savage Land* and *Princess and the Goblin.*

Contact: Dorian Langdon, senior vice president.

HOME FILM FESTIVAL

P.O. Box 2032
Scranton, PA 18501
Telephone: (800) 258-3456
Fax: (717) 344-3810

Home Film Festival is a video rental service which distributes foreign, American independent, and cult films.

Area(s) of specialty: Video rental

HUMAN RELATIONS MEDIA

175 Tomkins Avenue
Pleasantville, NY 10570
Telephone: (914) 769-6900
Fax: (914) 747-0839

Human Relations Media specializes in the production and distribution of health, guidance, math, and science video programs, covering a broad range of subjects. It seeks live-action video programming geared to the junior high and senior high curricula.

Area(s) of specialty: Programming for youth
Contact: Anton Schloal

INDEPENDENT VIDEO SERVICES

401 East 10th Avenue, Suite 160
Eugene, OR 97401-3317
Telephone: (503) 345-3455
Fax: (503) 345-5951

Independent Video Services is a small production and distribution company which looks for programs that "give back to society as a whole: education, especially health, overcoming disabilities, environmental, survivors and incest healing." The company can work on non-theatrical marketing of an existing program or production of a new video for national and international distribution. The company treats each product as a special case, with customized brochures, space advertising and mailings designed to reach particular segments of the marketplace. It sells to schools, hospitals, health care organizations, libraries, community groups, professional associations and government agencies. Its primary focus is on the U.S., but it also regularly sells to customers in Europe, Australia and Canada. The company generally prefers finished work, but it will look at scripts and respond to questions; it has collaborated on production projects for programs now in national and international distribution and can possibly arrange joint venture agreements. Some current titles in its library are *Big Dipper*; *We All Belong*; *Partners in Healing*; and *Relearning Touch.*

Year established: 1983

Area(s) of specialty: Health education

Company officers: Steve Christiansen, president, Gerald L. Joffe, secretary

Number of employees: 7

Contact: Bonnie B. Larson, operations manager

INTERAMA VIDEO CLASSICS

301 West 53rd Street, Suite 19E
New York, NY 10019
Telephone: (212) 977-4836
Fax: (212) 581-6582

Interama Video Classics, a "boutique" of uncut French classic subtitled films on video, distributes works by such filmmakers as Renoir, Pagnol, Blier, Melville, Resnais, Godard, Vadim, Grémillon, Demy, Rivette, Shoendoerffer, Girod, Bünuel, Bresson, Clouzot, Chabrol, and Genina. It also distributes some Spanish films and documentaries on African music, art and profiles. There are over 60 titles in its collection.

Year established: 1981

Area(s) of specialty: French films

Number of employees: 5

Contact: Nicole Jouve

INTERMEDIA

1300 Dexter Avenue North
Seattle, WA 98109
Telephone: (800) 553-8336
Fax: (206) 283-0778
e-mail: Shoff@lx.netcom.com

Intermedia specializes in distribution of social interest videos for the educational and corporate market. It is looking for "high quality programs that move quickly with a strong and clear educational message on topics of current social relevance." It serves a primarily non-theatrical/educational market, including schools, colleges and universities, public health departments, social service and government agencies, and corporations. Intermedia customizes a marketing plan around each program, using a telemarketing-based approach to successfully reach interested buyers. Depending upon the program, Intermedia may offer an advance against royalties or guarantee of sales. There are about 65 titles in its library, all of which are actively promoted and distributed; some current titles include *Hostages At Home; The Savage Cycle; Escape the Abuse* on domestic violence; *The Hidden Secret* on dating violence; *It Only Takes Once; Children Having Children; Know How* on teen pregnancy and teen sexuality; *Boys Will Be Boys; Don't Do It, Don't Allow It* on sexual harassment; *Coming 2; Picking Up The Pieces* on substance abuse; *Playing The Game;* and *Responding To Rape.*

Year established: 1981

Area(s) of specialty: Social issues

Company officers: Susan Hoffman, president, Ted Fitch, sales manager, Duke Pitak, operations manager

Number of employees: 18

Contact: Susan Hoffman

INTERNATIONAL CREATIVE EXCHANGE

3575 Cahuenga Blvd. West, Suite 475
Hollywood, CA 90068
Telephone: (213) 850-8080
Fax: (213) 850-8082

International Creative Exchange is a worldwide television/video and theatrical marketing and distribution company, which focuses on features and documentary series, particularly those geared toward family audiences. It carries over 2,000 hours of programming. Its program catalog contains television news/documentary series, documentary specials, travel/adventure series, current topic series, dramatic series, comedy series, music series, music specials, Shakespeare series, golden age of television series, children's television programming, and features (including family adventures, action thrillers, documentary features, and animated features). Several of its programs are also geared to the home video market. International Creative Exchange makes straight distribution deals. Many of its works are acquired through markets, screenings, and independent producer contacts. Its most important markets are domestic television pay, satellite, and cable (foreign and U.S. syndication), as well as home video (U.S., foreign license).

Year established: 1986

Area(s) of specialty: International television, family programs

Company officers: Olivier de Courson, president, Phill Catherall, vice president

Number of employees: 8

Contact: Phill Catherall

INTERNATIONAL FILM CIRCUIT

P.O. Box 1151
Old Chelsea Station
New York, NY 10011
Telephone: (212) 779-0660
Fax: (212) 779-9129

International Film Circuit was founded to tour curated packages of foreign films to the semi-theatrical market. It has evolved in the past ten years into a full service distribution company that serves the U.S. and Canadian theatrical, semi-theatrical and non-theatrical markets directly; and the home video and television markets through agents. The company specializes in target-marketing niche product to the theatrical and semi-theatrical markets, and looks for features and feature documentaries which will review well and which may have an identifiable and reachable target audience. Some of the releases it has handled include *Sex, Drugs and Democracy*; *In the Land of the Deaf*; *Anchoress*; *Halfaouine—Boy of the Terraces*; *The Garden*; *Night and Day*; and titles by Hou Hsiao-hsien and Raul Ruiz. The company has about 30 titles in its library.

Company officers: Wendy Lidell, president, Richard Peña, vice president, Ralph McKay, secretary
Area of specialty: Art house theatrical/university non-theatrical
Number of employees: 3
Year established: 1986
Contact: Wendy Lidell

INTERNATIONAL FILM FOUNDATION

155 West 72nd Street
New York, NY 10023
Telephone: (212) 580-1111

International Film Foundation distributes a library of 50 titles to the educational non-theatrical market.

Year established: 1945
Area(s) of specialty: Education, social studies.
Number of employees: 1-3
Contact: Sam Bryan

INTERNATIONAL VIDEO NETWORK

2246 Camino Ramon
San Ramon, CA 94583
Telephone: (510) 866-1344 x245
Fax: (510) 866-9262

International Video Network is a producer and distributor of travel, business, and consumer videos, distributing through several thousand retail locations, catalogs, marketing relationships with major publishing, travel, and entertainment companies.

Area(s) of specialty: Travel, business and consumer videos
Contact: Jenny Manocchio

IRS RELEASING

3520 Hayden Avenue
Culver City, CA 90232
(310) 838-7800
Fax: (310) 838-7402

IRS Releasing is an independent film production and distribution studio. Recent releases include *The Beans of Egypt, Maine*; and *Century*.

Contact: Seth M. Willenson, executive marketing consultant

ISA RELEASING, LTD.

680 North Lake Shore Drive, #1328
Chicago, IL 60611
Telephone: (312) 266-5900
Fax: (312) 266-1287

This new theatrical distribution company was started by the producers' representatives of *Hoop Dreams*. Its first release in 1995 was *Tie-Died: Rock 'n' Roll's Most Dedicated Fans*.

Area(s) of specialty: Feature film promotion and distribution
Company officers: John Iltis, principal, David Sikich, president
Number of employees: 2
Contact: David Sikich

ITALTOONS CORPORATION

32 West 40th Street, Suite 2L
New York, NY 10018
Telephone: (212) 730-0280
Fax: (212) 730-0313

Italtoons is an international producer and distributor of films and videos, specializing in the production and distribution of award-winning children's animation, a collection of European and American animated shorts for children, teenagers and adults, and the worldwide distribution of feature films for theatrical and other media. Italtoons can provide producers with sales, marketing and promotion; negotiation and execution of contracts and related documents; collection and followup of revenues; production and delivery of material to clients; and attendance at all major markets and frequent international sales trips. It is also a consultant buyer to several Italian television syndicators and theatrical distributors, and a North American consultant and coordinator for the ASIFA-Italy animation festival, Antennacinema CARTOON. The company has begun distribution and representation of programming on CD-ROM and other new media, and released five of its animated productions on an interactive educational

CD-ROM. Its theatrical releases include *Volere Volare; The Icicle Thief; Allegro Non Troppo;* and *The Tune;* animated and live-action co-productions include Mr. *Hiccup; Puppies and Kittens;* and *By Herself.* The company has also produced 15 half-hour animated classics for exhibition on cable specials, 4 half-hour animated specials for a children's pay television channel and coordinated the production of a short animated film *Help.*

Year established: 1978

Area(s) of specialty: Foreign and domestic distribution of animated films and video

Company officers: Giuliana Nicodemi, president

Number of employees: 4

Contact: Giuliana Nicodemi

ITC ENTERTAINMENT GROUP
12711 Ventura Blvd.
Studio City, CA 91604
(818) 760-2110
Fax: (818) 506-8189

ITC Entertainment Group produces and internationally distributes hundreds of features, made-for-television movies, dramas, documentaries, light entertainment, syndicated game shows, sport and musical specials, both acquisitions and its own productions. It looks for medium- to big-budget features and miniseries with stars and casts that have international appeal. The company is represented at all major markets and festivals. Some of its recent releases include *Fear of a Black Hat; The Last Seduction; Royce; Bon Appetit; Mama;* and *Prizzi's Family.*

Area of specialty: Theatrical features, television movies and miniseries

Year established: 1956

Contact: James Marrinan, senior executive vice president international

IVY FILM
PO Box 18376
Asheville, NC 28801
Telephone: (704) 285-9995
Fax: (704) 285-9997
e-mail: joshtager@aol.com

Ivy Film, a non-theatrical film distributor, has over 500 titles in its library, primarily entertainment features, documentaries, shorts and instructional films from around the world. The works in its catalog include madcap films, music, world's worst films, classics, film noir, documentaries, action and adventure, foreign features, golden age of television, vintage comedy, Charlie Chaplin, serials and short subjects. Its video releases include such works as *Breaking Into Hollywood; The Sorceress; Video Baby; Sexercise; The Naked City; Tamango; The Fighting Sullivans; Medea;* and *So Ends Our Night.*

It distributes to all markets—theatrical, non-theatrical, semi-theatrical, television (public, pay, syndication, cable)—domestically and internationally, utilizing sales agents in Europe, Latin America and Asia. Specially targeted film packages are releases on a quarterly basis, and its entire library is being targeted to the home video marketplace. Other target audiences are colleges, film societies, festivals, retrospective programs, and homages. Representatives attend MIPCOM, MIP, AFM, Berlin and Toronto. Ivy Classics Video produces, markets and distributes videos directly to educational and other non-theatrical markets. This line includes a "Novels on Film" Series.

Year established: 1972

Area(s) of specialty: Non-theatrical distribution, television, video

Company officers: Joshua Tager, vice president

Number of employees: 4

Contact: Joshua Tager

KINO INTERNATIONAL CORPORATION

333 West 39th Street, Suite 503
New York, NY 10018
Telephone: (212) 629-6880
Fax: (212) 714-0871

Kino International Corporation is a domestic theatrical and non-theatrical distributor of classic, independent and foreign films, and has over 300 films and 200 video features, shorts, and documentaries in its library. Its collection ranges from the earliest experiments in cinema and a wide selection of silent films to the newest films from around the world, with titles from six continents, over thirty countries, and in 23 languages. During the past few years, it has acquired and distributed theatrically or on video *Hyenas* (Senegal); *...and the earth did not swallow him* (U.S.); *The Day the Sun Turned Cold* (China); *Daughters of the Dust* (U.S.); *The Wonderful Horrible*

the best in world cinema

333 West 39th Street, Suite 503
New York, NY 10018
T: 212-629-6880 F: 212-714-0871

Life of Leni Riefenstahl (Germany); *The Blue Kite* (China); *Visions of Light* (U.S.); *La Vie de Boheme* (France); *Tito and Me* (Yugoslavia); *Paradjanov* (German); *Stefano Quantestori* (Italy); *Diabolique* (France); and *La Strada* (Italy). Its catalog also contains works by Martin Scorsese, Andrei Tarkovsky, Bertrand Tavernier, Chen Kaige, Sergei Eisenstein, Agnes Varda, John Huston, Akira Kurosawa, John Woo, Percy Adlon, Jiri Menzel, Bette Gordon, Ari Kaurismäki, Carl Franklin, Joel and Ethan Coen, and Derek Jarman. Kino is first and foremost a theatrical distributor, with non-theatrical, semi-theatrical, and home video being its next important markets. It has been particularly successful in targeting the general market for art films or with niche marketing for more targeted audiences (e.g., African-American audiences for *Daughters of the Dust* and Mexican Americans for *...and the earth did not swallow him*). Most of Kino's films are available in 16mm and 35mm and institutional/public performance video, and it has made new prints of several classics. In several cases, Kino can guarantee advances against royalties. Kino publishes two catalogs: Kino Nontheatrical and Kino on Video. Its representatives attend major festivals and markets to acquire films, and review films submitted on tape or via screenings.

Year established: 1977

Area(s) of specialty: Classic films, foreign films, U.S. independent films

Company officers: Donald Krim, president, Gary Palmucci, general manager

Number of employees: 10

Contact: Donald Krim, Gary Palmucci

THE KITCHEN VIDEO DISTRIBUTION COLLECTION

512 West 19th Street
New York, NY 10011
Telephone: (212) 255-5793
Fax: (212) 645-4258
e-mail: Kitchen@panix.com
WWW: http://www.panix.com/kitchen

The Kitchen Video Collection includes nearly 600 titles by almost 300 artists, assembled since 1975. The titles "give insight into the innovative experiments of the video medium and the history of the video vanguard" and are available internationally for rental, sale, broadcast and cablecast. The collection includes the early works of artists including Vito Acconci, Laurie Anderson, Robert Ashley, Charles Atlas, Dara Birnbaum, Abigail Child, Jem Cohen, Jeanne C. Finley, Shalom Gorewitz, Gary Hill, George Kuchar, Martha Rosler, John Sanborn, Richard Serra and Robert Wilson, as well as newer artists such as Kristine Diekman, Kathryn Greene, Van McElwee and Andreas Troeger. The catalog includes explanatory texts, running times, title and artist indexes, as well as complete purchase and rental information; it provides a reference and overview for those interested in the history of video art.

Year established: 1975

Area(s) of specialty: Video art, experimental, documentary

Contact: David Azarch/Cornelia Koch, media department

KJM3 ENTERTAINMENT GROUP, INC.

274 Madison Avenue, Suite 601
New York, NY 10016
Telephone: (212) 689-0950
Fax: (212) 689-6861
e-mail: KJM3274@aol.com

KJM3 Entertainment Group, Inc., specializes in the distribution and market-ing of film and television productions from throughout the African diaspora. Its overall goal is "to maintain a flow of films which speak to the diversity of experience in the African-American and world community, acknowledging the role of images in shaping and defining the way individuals and groups think about themselves." The company is "committed to the distribution of Black images and stories which interpret the complete spectrum of human experience." Based in New York City, KJM3 was formed by a group of African-American film and television professionals to provide distribution and marketing services to independent filmmakers, and the company is involved in theatrical and non-theatrical distribution and exhibition as well as distribution to television, home video and other markets. Its releases are marketed on a market-by-market basis, with a strategy which cross-refer-ences the tastes, habits and opinions of the African and African-American viewing audience in order to reach the broadest potential market. KJM3 debuted as distribution and marketing consultants on Julie Dash's *Daughters of the Dust* and has consulted on several other theatrical releases of films by African-American filmmakers. It has also released *The Man By The Shore* (Haiti), as well as *Neria* and *More Time* (Zimbabwe), *Gito L'Ingrat* (Burundi), and *Out of Sync*. KJM3 representatives attend many markets and festivals, including FESPACO, IFFM, MIP-TV, MIPCOM, and Cannes.

Year established: 1991

Area(s) of specialty: Distribution of films and videos from the African diaspora.

Company officers: Marlin Adams, vice president-business and legal affairs, Kathryn Bowser, vice president-administration, Michelle Materre, vice president-creative affairs, Mark Walton, vice president-sales and marketing.

Number of employees: 5

Contact: Michelle A. Materre

LANDMARK MEDIA

3450 Slade Run Drive
Falls Church, VA 22042
Telephone: (703) 241-2030/(800) 342-4336
Fax: (703) 536-9540

Landmark Media distributes to school, library and college markets, focusing on K-12 children's programming, science, and reading, language arts and social studies. Its contracts are exclusive.

Area(s) of specialty: Educational media

Company officers: Joan Hartogs, owner, Michael L. Hartogs, owner

Contact: Joan Hartogs

LEO FILM RELEASING

1509 N. Hoover, #1-2
Los Angeles, CA 90027
Telephone: (213) 913-3038
Fax: (213) 913-3038
e-mail: lustgarten@delphi.com

Leo Film Releasing distributes feature and some documentary films for all markets, including theatrical, foreign, television, and home video (its primary market). The company was formed as Lustgarten Entertainment Organization, to distribute in-house films, and has since expanded to encompass other producers' works. It is looking for names, and high quality for commercial audiences. It has 20 titles in its library, with 12 in active distribution, including *Risk*; *Trust Me*; *Peephole*; and *Astonished*.

Year established: 1991

Area(s) of specialty: Feature films

Company officers: Steve Lustgarten

Number of employees: 1

Contact: Steve Lustgarten

LIVE ENTERTAINMENT

15400 Sherman Way
Van Nuys, CA 91406-4211
Telephone: (818) 908-0303
Fax: (818) 778-3291

Live Entertainment is a domestic and international theatrical and home video/television licensing and multimedia distribution company. The company produces, develops and buys all rights, and gets involved in all stages of production; it is interested in films which already have a theatrical distributor for home video and other releases. Live actively seeks family films.

Company officers: Roger Burlage, CEO, Elliot Slutzky, executive vice president sales and marketing, Vincent Petrillo, vice president ancillary sales, Jim Steel, vice president, programming and acquisitions, Paul Almond, executive vice president, production and acquisitions.

LUCERNE MEDIA

37 Ground Pine Road
Morris Plains, NJ 07950
Telephone: (201) 538-1401/(800) 341-2293
Fax: (201) 538-0855

Lucerne Media is a marketing and distribution company which specializes in non-theatrical markets, including public and private schools, public libraries, colleges, health institutions, business and industry. The company executes a comprehensive advertising and promotion program; it has marketed the *Universal Video Yearbook* and *The Safe Child Program.*

Area(s) of specialty: Non-theatrical distribution

Company officers: Franklin J. Visco, president

Contact: Franklin J. Visco

MANBECK PICTURES CORPORATION

3621 Wakonda Drive
Des Moines, IA 50321-2132
Telephone: (515) 285-1166

Manbeck Pictures Corporation sells 16mm and videos of silent and sound productions, features and shorts (public domain).

Year established: 1966

Area(s) of specialty: Sales of 16mm films and videotapes

Contact: Earl "Buck" Manbeck, Jr.

MARYKNOLL WORLD PRODUCTIONS

Gonzaga Building
Maryknoll, NY 10545
Telephone: (914) 941-7590
Fax: (914) 762-0316

Maryknoll World Productions, with a current library of 29 titles, distributes documentary and educational films and videos, all of them handled individually with appropriate promotional activities. Distribution is to television (public, pay, network, satellite, cable), home video, public library systems and retail video outlets. Among the titles handled are *Consuming Hunger; From Sun Up; Gods of Metal;* and *Where There Is Hatred.* Many of Maryknoll's titles are independent works on Third World issues. In addition to national distribution, films and videos are distributed in Canada, Australia and Latin America.

Year established: 1911

Area(s) of specialty: Third World issues

Company officers: Fr. Donald J. Doherty, director, Michael Lavery, assistant director, Ronald E. Hines, promotions coordinator.

Contact: Fr. Donald J. Doherty

MCA/UNIVERSAL HOME VIDEO

70 Universal City Plaza
Universal City, CA 91608
Telephone: (818) 777-4300
Fax: (818) 733-1483

MCA/Universal Home Video releases major theatrical titles to the home video market, including classic Hollywood films, new titles from foremost filmmakers, and original programs. Its extensive catalog contains over 1,000 titles and laserdiscs, including action/adventure, children/family, comedy, drama, horror/sci-fi, instructional/fitness, music, mystery/suspense and western films on video.

Year established: 1980

Area(s) of specialty: Home video distribution

Company officers: Louis Feola, president, Andrew Kairey, senior vice president-marketing/sales, Blair Westlake, executive vice president-business affairs, Phil Pictaggi, senior vice president-operations

Number of employees: 130

Contact: Patti Jackson

MEDFILMS, INC.

6841 N. Cassim Place
Tucson, AZ 85704
Telephone: (602) 797-0345
Fax: (602) 742-6052

Medfilms produces and distributes programs on health care topics, including training videos on safety and compliance, including productions which address JCAHO, OSHA, and FDA requirements. Its markets include hospitals and other healthcare facilities.

Area(s) of specialty: Health and medical training videotapes

Contact: Alan Reeter, acquisitions

MEDIA GUILD

11722 Sorrento Valley Road, Suite E
San Diego, CA 92121
Telephone: (619) 755-9191/(800) 886-9196
Fax: (619) 755-4931

The Media Guild, a distributor of educational films and videos to non-theatrical markets, works with commercial producers and independent filmmakers. The range of topics in its library of over 200 titles includes the sciences, teenage subjects, AIDS, drugs and alcohol, family relationships, values, language arts, social studies, health issues, and guidance. The company contracts exclusively for all territories and markets, and its promotional activities include submitting all new titles for reviews, entering them in relevant film festivals, extensive convention and seminar coverage, direct mail promotions, special brochures, sales representation (including telemarketing). Discussion guides are included with all sales and rentals. About ten new productions are acquired each year; the company looks for films and videos which are useful in schools, libraries, institutions and health markets.

Year established: 1974

Area(s) of specialty: Instructional programs for education and health markets

Company officers: Preston Holdner, president

Number of employees: 12

Contact: Alicia Wahl, director of marketing

MEDIA METHODS

24097 North Shore Drive
Edwardsburg, MI 49112
Telephone: (616) 699-7061
Fax: (616) 699-7061
e-mail: Jmeuninck@aol.com

This company produces and distributes videos and books concerning alternative medicine, primarily natural health and primal medicine and Native American medicine. It is interested in broadcast-quality productions, mastered and original work on SVHS or better (no VHS originals), with content well organized, fast paced, how-to. Videos in its library include *Edible Wild Plants; One Hundred Useful Wild Herbs; Cooking with Edible Flowers; Trees Shrubs Nuts & Berries: A Forager's Guide; Natural Health with Medicinal Herbs and Healing Foods; Little Medicine; The Wisdom to Avoid Big Medicine.* Media Methods works only in video, no film, and primarily co-distributes. It will pay advances for large orders and co-distribution rights. It is tightly targeted to alternative medicine, feeling that independent producers in the same field stand the best chance. Libraries, schools, new agers and practitioners are the primary markets; the company distributes through traditional channels to these markets. It is negotiating with QVC and has sold its videos through many major catalogs.

Year established: 1975

Area(s) of specialty: Botanical medicine, medicinal herbs

Company officers: Jim Meuninck, president, Jill Meuninck, vice president/treasurer

Number of employees: 3

Contact: Jim Meuninck

MERRIMACK FILMS

22D Hollywood Avenue
Ho-Ho-Kus, NJ 07423
Telephone: (201) 652-1989
Fax: (201) 652-1973

This company distributes films on labor to colleges, unions, governmental agencies, and businesses. It views all submissions for use in the academic market. Its target audience for its works (the library contains seven works) is college, professional, and adult. Some titles are *Loose Bolts; Crisis Bargaining; Givebacks; Union Democracy; Unions in Crisis.*

Year established: 1983

Area(s) of specialty: Labor relations, economics

Company officers: Henry Bass, president

Contact: Henry Bass

MILESTONE FILM AND VIDEO, INC.

275 West 96th Street, Suite 28C
New York, NY 10025
Telephone: (212) 865-7449
Fax: (212) 222-8952
e-mail: MileFilms@aol.com

Milestone Film and Video was founded in 1990 to bring out the best of old and new films. Its re-releases have included restored versions of Visconti's *Rocco and His Brothers*; Murnau's *Tabu* and *The Last Laugh*; Schoedsack's *Grass* and *Chang*; Antonioni's *Red Desert* ; and Buñuel's *The Young One*. The company's new releases have included the films of Eleanor Antin; documentaries of Philip Haas; Wenders's *Notebook on Cities and Clothes*; Yong-kyun's *Why Has Bodhi-Dharma Left for the East?*; and Besson's *Atlantis*. Milestone is also known for rediscovering, acquiring and distributing unknown classics that have never been available in the U.S. and Canada, including Pasolini's *Mamma Roma*; Hitchcock's *Bon Voyage* and *Aventure Malgache*; Kalatozov's *I Am Cuba*; and Campion's *Two Friends*. The company has approximately 100 films in current distribution. It is seeking "quality films and videos from the present and the past that challenge the viewer at the same time they entertain." Acquisitions have included features, documentaries, and foreign language films, "works of great intelligence and emotional power"; acquisitions are from a variety of sources, including festivals, archives, word-of-mouth and research.

Year established: 1990

Number of employees: 3

Company officers: Amy Heller, president, Dennis Doros, vice-president.

Area of specialty: American independent, foreign and classic films and videos

Contact: Amy Heller, Dennis Doros

MIRAMAX FILMS

375 Greenwich Street
New York, NY 10013
Telephone: (212) 941-3800
Fax: (212) 941-3949

Miramax Films has cultivated a reputation as an effective distributor of independent specialty adult films, many of which have become award-winning successes through aggressive marketing and non-traditional publicity campaigns. It acquires films which are considered too offbeat for major studios and works out a strong marketing plan, taking an individual approach with each film's advertising and publicity campaigns. Producers and directors are frequently strongly involved in the distribution experience, including doing many interviews and traveling to promote the film (after the success of *Pulp Fiction*, Miramax granted director Quentin Tarantino a division within the company). Its purchase in 1993 by the Walt Disney Company provided the company with a strong base. Its 1995 release slate included 40 films, including works such as *The Innocent; Belle de Jour; Smoke; Il Postino; The Prophecy; Kids* (for which Miramax formed a special unit, Shining Excalibur Films, to distribute the film when it could not be handled by Disney due to its NC-17 rating); *Unzipped*; and *The Glass Shield*. Some of its major successes include *Pulp Fiction; The Piano; Cinema Paradiso; My Left Foot*; and *The Crying Game*.

Year established: 1979

Area(s) of specialty: Independent specialty films

Company officers: Harvey Weinstein, co-chairman, Bob Weinstein, co-chairman, Eamonn Bowles, senior vice president and president, Shining Excalibur, Donna Daniels, senior vice president, communication, Donna Gigliotti, executive vice president, Mark Gill, president of marketing, Marcy Granata, executive vice president, marketing and publicity, Mark Tusk, vice president, acquisitions, Agnes Mentre, president, Miramax Zo˜89, vice president of acquisitions and co-productions, Cynthia Swartz, senior vice president, special projects, Paul Rosenberg, senior vice president of production, David Linde, executive vice president, Miramax International, Richard Sands, president, Miramax International

Contact: Amy Israel, director of acquisitions

MLR FILMS INTERNATIONAL

301 East 62nd Street
New York, NY 10021
Telephone: (212) 759-1729
Fax: (212) 759-8375

This company distributes features, documentaries (educational series), television series, and American classic films. Representatives attend MIP-TV, MIPCOM, Cannes, MIFED, AFM, NATPE, and IFFM. Its film library contains 800 titles.

Year established: 1991

Area(s) of specialty: Theatrical, television, video licensing worldwide

Company officers: Alan Miller, Nancy Miller

Number of employees: 2

Contact: Alan Miller

ARTHUR MOKIN PRODUCTIONS, INC.

P.O. Box 232
Santa Rosa, CA 95402
Telephone: (707) 542-4868
Fax: (707) 542-6182

Arthur Mokin Productions, Inc., handles about 250 films and videos designed for the educational market, particularly K-12, math, science, social studies and language arts. Primary markets include schools, libraries, and home video. It has built up its customer and media contact list over several years. The company accepts documentary and narrative shorts, animated, sports, health/medical, scientific and television productions. It distributes to non-theatrical, television and home video markets, on an exclusive basis; Canada, Asia, Australia and Europe are also covered using foreign agents.

Year established: 1966

Area(s) of specialty: Educational, K-12, gardening

Company officers: Bill Mokin, Dona Mokin

Number of employees: 3

Contact: Bill Mokin

MULTIMEDIA ENTERTAINMENT, INC.

45 Rockefeller Plaza, 35th Floor
New York, NY 10111
Telephone: (212) 332-2000
Fax: (212) 332-2010

Multimedia Entertainment, a television production and distribution company, distributes feature and short programs for television, including such programs as *Donahue*; *Sally Jessy Raphael*; *Jerry Springer*; *Rush Limbaugh*; *The Television Show*; *Susan Powter*; *Dennis Prager*; *Newstalk Television* (24-hour cable network).

Year established: 1977

Area(s) of specialty: Talk shows

Company officers: Robert Turner, president, Richard C. Coveny, executive vice president, Richard Thrall, senior vice president, programming, Burt Dubrow, vice president, programming

Number of employees: 65

MUSEUM OF MODERN ART-CIRCULATING FILM AND VIDEO LIBRARY

11 West 53rd Street
New York, NY 10019
Telephone: (212) 708-9530
Fax: (212) 708-9531

The Museum of Modern Art's Circulating Film and Video Library has over 1200 films and videos which span the history of cinema. The collection includes feature films (mainly early silent works), documentaries, experimental works, video production and animated films. Its strengths are European and American cinema of the silent period, avant garde, documentary and British independent and Canadian film. Its extensively annotated catalog provides several cross indexes. The Hans Richter estate has provided ongoing support for the acquisition of works by independent filmmakers.

Year established: 1935

Contact: Bill Sloan

MYPHEDUH FILMS, INC.

403 K Street, NW
Washington, DC 20001
Telephone: (202) 289-6677
Fax: (202) 289-4477

Mypheduh Films, Inc., distributes features and documentaries by African and African-American independent filmmakers, theatrically and non-theatrically. It was founded to "create a channel for African and African-American filmmakers to express themselves; to be able to freely project the images, experiences, struggles and various lifestyles of Africans in the diaspora and on the continent by independent filmmakers that are of and about their people's welfare." It seeks works with quality story lines and developed characters that project realistic images of African descendants. In 1994-95, it had a stunning theatrical success with the release of *Sankofa*, which was four-walled in cities across the country and drew huge audiences, followed by the video release of the film. Its library also includes several works by Haile Gerima, including *Wilmington 10-U.S.A 10,000; Ashes and Embers; Harvest 3,000 Years; Child of Resistance* and *Bush Mama*; as well as such films as *Peasant Letter; Losing Ground; Killer of Sheep; Wend Kuuni; Parcel Post; Shadow of the Earth; Passing Through; Brick by Brick; Camera d'Afrique; House Arrest*; and *The Cruz Brothers and Miss Malloy*.

Year established: 1978

Area(s) of specialty: African and African-American films by independent filmmakers

Company officers: Haile Gerima, Shirikiana Gerima

Number of employees: 6

Contact: Shirikiana Gerima

MYRIAD PICTURES

8899 Beverly Blvd., Suite 909
Los Angeles, CA 90048
Telephone: (310) 550-7588
Fax: (310) 550-1009

Formerly Videfilm Producers International, Myriad Pictures sells to television and home video markets in the U.S. and abroad in all territories. Its programs include music and variety, theatre for television, contemporary drama, musical biographies, feature films, family programs, and documentaries. It also has several feature, dramatic and documentary programs in development. Representatives attend MIPCOM, Monte Carlo, MIP-TV, Cannes, IFFM, AFM, and NATPE. Some of the approximately 50 titles it distributes are *Chick Corea and Band; Miles Ahead: The Music of Miles Davis; Nancy Wilson and Band; A Night of Jazz: Live at Sweet Basil; Aretha Franklin: Queen of Soul; James Brown and His Very Special Guest B.B. King; The Temptations Live in Concert; Bill Monroe: Father of Bluegrass Music; Deep Blues; Heifitz; Andy Warhol—Made in China; Drawing the Line: A Portrait of Keith Haring; Miro—The Light of Majorca; Cage/Cunningham; Everybody Dance Now; Honi Coles, The Class Act of Tap; Flashing on the Sixties— A Tribal Document; Lodz Ghetto;* and *Partisans of Vilna.*

Year established: 1988

Area(s) of specialty: General programming

Company officers: Kirk D'Amico, president

Number of employees: 3

Contact: Sophie Boller-Reardon

MYSTIC FIRE VIDEO

P.O. Box 422
New York, NY 10012-0008
Telephone: (800) 999-1319/(212) 941-0999
Fax: (212) 941-1443
e-mail: mysticfire@echonyc.com
WWW: http://www.mysticfire.com/~mysticfire

Mystic Fire video specializes in works for the home video and institutional markets concerned with "the physical manifestations of mind and spirit," with "ideas and emotions as they find their expression in the body and through the arts." With over 190 titles in its catalog, Mystic Fire's videos cover subject areas including transformative visions, healing and consciousness, native peoples, relationships, literati, ancient cultures, society in chaos, cinema, art, music and dance. Some of its newer titles include *Explorations into Consciousness: An Interview with Deepak Chopra; Henry Miller Odyssey; Anaïs Observed; Secret Egypt; Sex and the Sacred: A Conversation with Sam Keen; Dance & Myth: The World of Jean Erdman; Willem de Kooning;* and *The World of Buckminster Fuller.*

Year established: 1985

Area(s) of specialty: Arts, avant-garde, documentary

Number of employees: 8

Contact: Bill Breeze

NAATA/CROSS CURRENT MEDIA

National Asian American Telecommunications Association
346 Ninth Street, 2nd Floor
San Francisco, CA 94103
Telephone: (415) 552-9550
Fax: (415) 863-7428

NAATA is a media arts service organization whose mission is to advance the ideals of cultural pluralism in America and to promote better understanding of the Asian Pacific American experience. It is one of five National Minority Consortia created to provide programming to the Public Broadcasting Service, for which it acquires, packages and distributes television and radio programs that are representative of Asian American experiences. As a distributor, it focuses on documentary/educational, narrative, and experimental works which should reflect the Asian diaspora experience. Most of its titles are marketed to schools and universities, libraries, and other educational institutions, film festivals and special exhibitions. Many of its acquisitions come through NAATA's International Asian American Film Festival in San Francisco, as well as through submissions from independent producers. Target audiences include high school, college and up, with focus on Asian American and ethnic studies and multicultural programs; NAATA's markets also include museums and other educational institutions that program ethnic works. Foreign markets include Canadian educational and potential television as well as potential Asian television. It has included many first productions in its collections and is interested in work geared toward teenagers. NAATA will preview works-in-progress and rough cuts, and will pay for all dubs, jackets, and marketing materials. Advances are given in some cases. Some current titles in its catalog are *Bui Doi: Life Like Dust; Carved in Silence; The Color of Honor; Days of Waiting; The Fall of the I-Hotel; Jazz Is My Native Language; Maxine Hong Kingston: Talking Story; Shadow Over Tibet: Stories in Exile; Sa-I-Gu: From Korean Women's Perspectives; Yuri Kochiyama: Passion for Justice; Momiji: Japanese Maple;* and *Sakako and the Thousand Paper Cranes.* In 1995, the library featured 117 titles, with 106 currently being distributed.

Year established: 1980

Area(s) of specialty: Asian American and Asian film and video

Company officers: Deann Borshay, executive director, Pamela Matsuoka, distribution manager, Janice Sakamoto, broadcast program director

Number of employees: 10

Contact: Pamela Matsuoka, Elsa Eder

NATIONAL BLACK PROGRAMMING CONSORTIUM

929 Harrison Avenue, Suite 101
Columbus, OH 43215
Telephone: (614) 299-5355
Fax: (614) 299-4761

The National Black Programming Consortium, one of CPB's Minority Consortia, distributes not only to PBS stations but also to schools, organizations, and individuals to create a greater awareness of films and videos addressing issues relevant to Black people. Some recently distributed productions include *Street of Dreams; Ethnic Notions; Mandela; X The Baby Cinema; Black Frontier Series*; and *Black Vintage Film Series*. Since its founding, it has distributed over 1,000 programs to PBS stations, other telecommunications entities, and educational institutions; distribution to educators has increased to answer a growing interest in using film and video as part of classroom curricula. NBPC also administers a program development fund, which provides financial support from $1,000-$50,000, for film and video programs that "embrace and promote the experiences and perspectives of Black people"; over 70 programs have been funded and have appeared on PBS's core schedule and on major strand series such as *American Playhouse, The American Experience*, and *P.O.V.*

Year established: 1980

Area of specialty: Programming addressing issues relevant to Black people.

Contact: John Patterson

NATIONAL GEOGRAPHIC TELEVISION

1145 17th Street, NW
Washington, DC 20036-4688
Telephone: (202) 857-7680
Fax: (202) 775-6590

National Geographic Television, a wholly owned subsidiary of the National Geographic Society, focuses on documentary production and works with a number of filmmakers. It produces over 60 hours of programming each year for its *National Geographic Specials*, broadcast on NBC and *National Geographic Explorer*, broadcast on TBS. National Geographic Video represents the documentary series. These series are internationally presented in a joint venture documentary distribution deal with London's Explore International. NGT searches internationally for documentary programming which fits in with the series profile, considering a wide range of subjects, including "adventure and exploration films, films that tell stories of people around the world whose lifestyles or activities are particularly exotic, unusual or noteworthy, and non-fiction children's material." NGT Acquisitions considers only completed films and pre-buys on promising films in production.

Year established: 1965

Area(s) of specialty: Documentary series

Contact: Jenny Apostol, head of acquisitions

NEW AND UNIQUE VIDEOS

2336 Sumac Drive
San Diego, CA 92105
Telephone: (619) 282-6126
Fax: (619) 283-8264
e-mail: videoduo@aol.com

New and Unique Videos handles "special interest" videos (educational, how-to, documentary, sports, health, fitness, etc. The company is looking for video acquisitions which are produced on high-quality video (e.g., Betacam SP) with professionally designed box covers, ready for marketing. New and Unique Videos has also produced 12 titles, which it distributes along with videos by other independent producers. Home video is its top market; its videos are for individuals who want to create an educational video library. Primary acquisition methods include conventions and submissions from independent producers. New and Unique Videos gets commissions and/or royalties for titles placed and sold domestically and via foreign rights deals. The company has also been successful in gaining sponsorship for its video titles. Some of its titles include *Full Cycle: World Odyssey*; *John Howard's Lessons in Cycling*; *Ultimate Mountain Biking*; *The Great Mountain Biking Video*; *Massage for Relaxation*; *Common Sense Self-Defense for Women*; *Soaring in a Sailplane*; *Steppin' Out: Ultimate Interval-Training System*; and *California Big Hunks*.

Year established: 1982

Area(s) of specialty: Production and distribution of special interest video titles

Company officers: Mark Schulze, Patricia Mooney

Contact: Mark Schulze

NEW DAY FILMS

22D Hollywood Avenue
Ho-Ho-Kus, NJ 07423
Telephone: (201) 652-6590
Fax: (201) 652-1973

New Day Films is a self-distribution cooperative of independent producers of educational films, television productions, and social issue or personal films who govern and manage the company. Individual members carry out specific functions within the co-op and participate in group decision making. It was founded by emerging producers for the distribution of their work. The co-op continues to include and accept films and videos by newcomers as well as veteran independent producers. Films and videos cover a wide range of topics: gender and socialization, cultural studies, health, the environment, young adult issues, birth, parenting and families, urban and community experience, U.S. labor and social history, international concerns. Generally, New Day finds new work through submissions from independent producers interested in self-distribution. Co-op members are readily accessible sources of information about New Day and frequently serve as the initial conduits of information for film and video makers seeking an alternative to traditional nontheatrical distributors. Distribution, exclusive throughout the U.S. only, is to non-theatrical markets. Individual members have other arrangements for foreign and television distribution of their work. Co-op members are responsible for and usually produce all individual and group promotional material. Members share costs for production of a biannual catalog, catalog supplements and direct-mail brochures promoting groups of films to highly segmented markets. New release announcements, awards, press releases and other publicity about the entire co-op are usually produced by a promotion committee. New Day regularly prepares promotional material about related groups of titles (e.g., about young adult issues, U.S. social history, art, global perspectives) to highly targeted markets. Regular mailings, telemarketing, conference attendance and special promotions are among New Day activities. There are approximately 50 members in the co-op (active, semi-active and classic) and close to 100 titles in the collection. Some of the titles are *Union Maids*; *With Babies and Banners*; *Breaking Silence: The Story of the Sisters at Desales Heights*; *If the Mango Tree Could Speak*; *Dear Lisa: A Letter to My Sister*; *Funny Ladies: A Portrait of Women Cartoonists*; *Style Wars*; *Growing Up Female*; *Finding Our Way*; *Am I Normal?*; *Godzilla Meets Mona Lisa*; *All Under Heaven*; *Leona's Sister Gerri*; *Twitch and Shout*; *Do Not Enter: The Visa War Against Ideas*; and *Hope: Songs of the Fourth World*. An information packet about cooperative self-distribution through New Day, as well as details about application procedures, can be obtained from New York member Ralph Arlyck.

Year established: 1972

Area(s) of specialty: Social issue and social change film and video

Number of employees: 1

Contact: Ralph Arlyck, 79 Raymond Avenue, Poughkeepsie, NY 12601; tel: (914) 485-8489

NEW DIMENSION MEDIA INC.

85803 Lorane Highway
Eugene, OR 97405
Telephone: (503) 484-7125
Fax: (503) 485-5267

New Dimension Media specializes in promoting independently produced documentaries through customized distribution. Its focus is extensive personalized contacts and a telephone-intensive preview booking system which gets media librarians and audio-visual personnel to preview programs. The staff travels over 100,000 miles a year to media centers, major trade conferences and state preview seminars to visit major customers. In addition, the company does direct-mail campaigns and employs a telephone marketing system that targets and saturates the major non-theatrical markets, including educators, public librarians, health groups, social service agencies, and church groups. Its database includes over 15,000 media educators and audio-visual librarians that purchase film and video programs. It keeps active titles limited in order to give each program specialized attention. Releases include productions in such subject areas as Academy Award nominations/winners/nominees, adolescent heath and welfare, African studies, aging, agriculture/soil science/farming, AIDS/STDs, alcohol/substance abuse, American social issues, anatomy, animals/nature, anthropology, art/music/dance, astronomy/space, authors, auto safety, biography, biology, business/business education, child abuse, child development, computers/technology, conservation, cultural studies, current issues, death and dying, disabilities, ecology/environment, economics, entomology, forestry, geography, geology, gerontology, guidance and values, health, history, home economics, international studies, language arts/literature, mental health, multicultural, music, Native American studies, Pacific Northwest studies, parenting, poetry/poets, pregnancy, safety, science, self esteem, sexuality, social studies, television.

Year established: 1979

Area(s) of specialty: Non-theatrical distribution

Company officers: Steve Raymen

Number of employees: 9

Contact: Steve Raymen

NEW LINE CINEMA

888 Seventh Avenue, 20th Floor
New York, NY 10106
Telephone: (212) 649-4900
Fax: (212) 649-4966

New Line Cinema is a leading publicly held independent producer and distributor of theatrical films and television productions, with offices in New York, Los Angeles, Chicago, Atlanta, and Dallas. Its library includes a diverse array of genre and specialty films: comedy, cult, horror, art, action, foreign, and fantasy. The company includes in-house theatrical, distribution, marketing, home video, television, acquisitions, production, licensing and merchandising divisions. Its subsidiaries include New Line Productions, Fine Line Features (the company's arthouse, specialty film arm), New Line International, New Line Home Video, New Line Television, and New Line Licensing and Merchandising. New Line began as a cult movie distributor to college campuses and film societies in the 1970s (with such films as *The Seduction of Mimi* and *Reefer Madness*), and moved into niche and horror films in the 1980s. The company built its reputation and foundation as a successful company on such films as *Nightmare on Elm Street*; *House Party*; *Teenage Mutant Ninja Turtles*; *Torch Song Trilogy*;

Smithereens; Polyester; Pink Flamingos; Texas Chainsaw Massacre; and *Metropolitan.* Recent releases include *The Mask; Seven; Mortal Kombat;* and *Now and Then.* Future releases include *The Long Kiss Goodnight; The Island of Dr. Moreau; Gundown!; Bed of Roses; Rumble in the Bronx; The Grass Harp; Frankie Starlight; Feeling Minnesota; The Mask 2; The Women;* and *Lost in Space.* In 1994, the company was purchased by TBS. Los Angeles office: 116 North Robertson Blvd., #200, Los Angeles, CA 90048; (310) 854-5811; fax: (310) 854-1824.

Area(s) of specialty: Theatrical motion picture distribution

Company officers: Robert Shaye, chairman and CEO, Michael Lynne, president and COO, Sara Risher, chairman, New Line Productions, Mitch Goldman, president, marketing and distribution, Ruth Vitale, Fine Line, Amy Henkels, vice president of production and development, Sasha Emerson, senior vice president, television production and development, Camela Galano, senior vice president, international sales and marketing, Marjorie Lewis, vice president, creative affairs, Rolf Mittweg, president, New Line International, Nestor Nieves, senior vice president, international sales and administration, Mark Ordesky, vice president acquisitions and co-productions.

NEW YORKER FILMS

16 West 61st Street
New York, NY 10023
Telephone: (212) 247-6110
Fax: (212) 307-7855

New Yorker Films specializes in the domestic distribution of international theatrical feature films and theatrical shorts, including many film classics. Some of the titles in its catalog are *Babette's Feast; Bagdad Cafe; Chocolat; Frida; La Lectrice; Powaqatsi; Red Sorghum; Voices of Sarafina!; Sand and Blood; Guelwaar; I Can't Sleep;* and *Yaaba.* Most of its releases come from Asia, Africa, Latin America and Eastern Europe. In 1989 it launched its domestic home video division, which selects its titles from among the more than 400 works in its collection, including classics by filmmakers such as Bertolucci, Fassbinder, and Herzog. The company is also associated with the Lincoln Square Cinemas.

Year established: 1964

Area(s) of specialty: International theatrical feature films and shorts

Company officers: Dan Talbot

Contact: Dan Talbot

NITECLUB VIDEO/ODDBALL FILM AND VIDEO

P.O. Box 425481
San Francisco, CA 94142-5481
Telephone: (415) 558-8112
Fax: (415) 863-9771

Niteclub Video/Oddball Film and Video distributes primarily "new, cutting-edge" erotic features and shorts of all sexual persuasions. It looks for "strong, well-developed ideas that challenge contemporary ideas of sexuality." Among the dozen or so titles in its collection are *Photosex; Mistress Kay's Bedtime Story*; and *A Dysfunctional Fairy Tale*. Its collection is aimed primarily at the home video market for mid 20s-40s independent viewers.

Year established: 1982

Area(s) of specialty: Experimental, erotic

Company officers: Stephen Parr

Number of employees: 4

Contact: Stephen Parr

NORTHERN ARTS ENTERTAINMENT, INC.

Northern Arts Studios
Williamsburg, MA 01096
Telephone: (413) 268-9301
Fax: (413) 268-9309

Founded by filmmakers John Lawrence Ré and David Mazor, Northern Arts Entertainment "believes in working closely with filmmakers," "is not afraid of provocative, controversial films" and believes "that creative marketing and strict cost control is the key to the best possible return for both producer and distributor." The company distributes films theatrically, as well as to non-theatrical, semi-theatrical, home video and television markets. It may provide completion funding, negative pickups, advances, and guarantees. With 28 films in its library, some of the successful titles handled by Northern Arts include *Tokyo Decadence; Brian Wilson: I Just Wasn't Made For These Times; Chameleon Street; Dirty Money; Raining Stones; Temptation of a Monk; Luna Park*; and *Stepping Razor*. It is looking for high quality, American independent and foreign films.

Year established: 1989

Area(s) of specialty: Art and specialty films

Company officers: John Lawrence Ré, chairman, David Mazor, president, Alison Brantley, vice president, acquisitions, Jacqueline Sheridan, acquisitions

Number of employees: 6

Contact: Jacqueline Sheridan

OCTOBER FILMS

65 Bleecker Street, 2nd Floor
New York, NY10012
Telephone: (212) 539-4000
Fax: (212) 539-4099

October Films is an specialized film distribution company which handles North American distribution of independent features. Some of its recent releases include *Life is Sweet; Tous Les Matins du Monde; Kika; The Last Seduction; Colonel Chabert* and *Search and Destroy*. Its non-theatrical catalog lists a wealth of independent feature productions, including such works as *Red Firecracker, Green Firecracker; Dance Black America; The War Room; Bad Behavior; The Living End; A Room With a View; Cage/Cunningham; Yeelen; Salaam Bombay; Return of the Secaucus 7; Life is Sweet; Comic Book Confidential; Say Amen Somebody; El Norte; Rosalie Goes Shopping; The Brother From Another Planet* and *Tea in the Harem*.

Area(s) of specialty: Feature film distribution

Company officers: Bingham Ray, co-managing executive, John Schmidt, co-managing executive, Amir Malin, co-managing executive, Michael Silberman, vice president, theatrical distribution, Susan Glatzer, director of acquisitions, Linda Duchin, non-theatrical

Contact: Susan Glatzer

ORIGINAL CINEMA

419 Park Avenue South, 20th floor
New York, NY 10016
Telephone: (212) 545-0177
Fax: (212) 685-2625

Original Cinema is a domestic distributor of specialized theatrical films, particularly low-budget, high-quality independent productions. Some of the films it has handled include *A Taxing Woman; Repeat Dive; Tetsuo: The Iron Man; Feed; The Smile of the Lamb; Laser Man; First Date;* and *Through the Wire*. With a small number of acquisitions, it is able to map out regional and national distribution strategies in key cities. Promotional activities include the use of outside publicists; it provides exhibitors and publicists with information and promotional material as needed.

Year established: 1988

Area(s) of specialty: Fiction features, documentary features

Company officers: Tom Prassis, vice president, marketing and distribution, Liz Empleton Jenkins, vice president, acquisitions, Elliott Kanbar, vice president, business affairs, Alexandra White, vice president, development

Number of employees: 15

Contact: Liz Empleton Jenkins

ORION PICTURES – CLASSIC DIVISION

1888 Century Park East
Los Angeles, CA 90272
Telephone: (310) 282-0550
Fax: (310) 282-9902

Orion Classics, a division of Orion Pictures, handles the worldwide production and distribution of specialty independent films to theatrical, non-theatrical and home video markets. Some of the titles in its collection are

Jeffrey; Bar Girls; Au Revoir Les Enfants; Babette's Feast; A Great Wall; Ran; Another Country; End of the Line; and *Mystery Train.*
Area(s) of specialty: Theatrical feature films
Contact: Leon Falk, acquisitions

OUTSIDER ENTERPRISES

2940 16th Street, Suite 200-1
San Francisco, CA 94103
Telephone: (415) 863-0611
Fax: (415) 863-0611

Outsider Enterprises was started by filmmaker Marc Huestis and co-producer Lawrence Helman during the self-distribution of the film *Sex Is...*, which became one of the year's top grossing documentaries through an aggressive grassroots and four-walling campaign. Since then it has distributed that film and *Young At Hearts*, as well as providing publicity services for *Dialogues With Madwomen; Highway of Heartache; Ballot Measure 9; Complaints of a Dutiful Daughter;* and *Fast Trip, Long Drop.* Outsider is looking for films that can play theatrically, either new or festival film favorites that cannot find traditional film distribution. The company also does films that can be pitched to both domestic and foreign television. It is capable of taking on 4-5 films per year and pushing them heavily through grassroots and all media campaigns, targeted at specific audiences. Outsider will look at works-in-progress and rough cuts, given filmmakers' realistic goals about the theatrical potential of their productions. For acquisitions, Outsider representatives attend festivals and film markets, solicit tapes from festival catalogs and follow up on recommendations.
Year established: 1993
Area(s) of specialty: Independent films
Company officers: Marc Huestis, Lawrence Helman
Number of employees: 2
Contact: Marc Huestis, Lawrence Helman

OVERSEAS FILMGROUP

8800 Sunset Blvd., Suite 302
Los Angeles, CA 90069
Telephone: (310) 855-1199
Fax: (310) 855-0719

Overseas Filmgroup is a worldwide sales and distribution company, which specializes in a range of independent feature films; it acts as a domestic and foreign sales agent, representing independent feature films for cable, network, worldwide, non-theatrical and home video markets. The company acquires the rights to 10-15 films per year. Representatives attend several major markets each year. Offices are in Los Angeles, Rome and London. The company's domestic theatrical division, First Look Pictures, focuses on new and specialty films. Some of its releases include *Infinity; The Secret of Roan Inish; God's Army; The Unbelievable Truth; Medium Straight; A Soldier's Tale; Blood and Sand;* and *Runaway Dreams.*

Year established: 1980

Area(s) of specialty: International independent feature film distribution

Company officers: Robert Little, chairman, Ellen Little, president, Maud Nadler, director, creative affairs

Contact: Maud Nadler

PACIFIC ISLANDERS IN COMMUNICATIONS

1221 Kapiolani Blvd., #6A-4
Honolulu, HI 96814
(808) 591-0059
Fax: (808) 591-1114
e-mail: piccom@elele.peacesat.hawaii.edu.

Pacific Islanders in Communications recently started its distribution arm and is in the process of building its debut catalog, which will be released in the spring of 1996. Its emphasis is work that is produced from a Pacific Islander perspective (Polynesian, Micronesian, etc.) for public television and the cable television and non-theatrical markets. Established in 1991, PIC is a national nonprofit media arts organization established primarily to increase national public broadcast programming by and about Pacific Islanders, programming which "fosters a deeper understanding of the values inherent in Pacific Island cultures and which enhances public recognition of and appreciation for Pacific Islanders." PIC is funded by the Corporation for Public Broadcasting. There are about eight titles currently in its library, including *Pacific Diaries* series, *Storytellers* series, and *Act of War: The Overthrow of the Hawaiian Monarchy.*

Year established: 1991

Area of specialty: Pacific Islander films and videos, narrative and documentary

Company officers: Carol Ann Ibanez, president, board of directors.

Number of employees: 5

Contact: Lurline Wailana McGregor, executive director

PANORAMA ENTERTAINMENT CORPORATION

125 North Main Street
Port Chester, NY 10573
Telephone: (914) 937-1603
Fax: (914) 937-8496

Panorama Entertainment Corporation handles features and documentaries for domestic theatrical release, international distribution, and non-theatrical distribution. It does not seek to compete with the major independent distributors, but looks for a niche or spark in a film that it can exploit. Each film is marketed independently and "becomes more important than either the filmmaker or distributor." Deals are tailored to the product and the rights available. Panorama looks for product which it feels it can market and adapts it to a particular market and/or audience. It will look at works-in-progress and absolutely consider works which are risky. Some of the titles in its library are *Public Access; Shotgun Wedding; Ride to Wounded Knee; Talk 16; When Pigs Fly; Silent Witness; Kissy Cousins Monster Babies;* and *Odile and Evette.*

Year established: 1986

Area(s) of specialty: Theatrical distribution of niche films

Company officers: Stuart Strutin, president, Steve Florin, vice president

Number of employees: 3

Contact: Steve Florin

PAPER TIGER TELEVISION

339 Lafayette Street
New York, NY 10012
Telephone: (212) 420-9045
Fax: (212) 420-8223
WWW: http://flicker.com/orgs/papertiger

Founded over a decade ago, Paper Tiger's mission is "to work for greater democratization of the communications industry." Its programs are cablecast on Manhattan's public access channels designed for community use. The Paper Tiger collection of over 240 titles "analyzes and challenges the mainstream media" and is used by libraries, universities, community and arts organizations. Many of the programs examine a particular aspect of the communications industry, from print media to television and movies, looking at its impact on public perception and cultural life; other videos represent people and views absent from mainstream media. Paper Tiger has recently produced a series of programs about the information highway, communications policy and access to such resources. Titles in its catalog also cover such topics as advertising, Central/South America, international politics, labor, news and information, pop culture/images, youth and women. Some of its most popular titles include *Ads! Ads! Ads!; Animals in Mass Media: Images of a Schizophrenic Society; The Bicentennial Will Not Be Televised; Born to be Sold: Martha Rosler Reads the Strange Case of Baby M S; Brian Winston Reads TV News; CBS Tries the NY3: Racist Lies on Prime-time TV; Collateral Damage; Desperately Seeking Reality: Herb Schiller Reads Trash TV; The Gulf Crisis TV Project; Drawing the Line at Pittston;* and *Felt Evidence: Investigating Reproductive Technologies.*

Year established: 1978

Area(s) of special: Television and video, media critique

Contact: Cyrille Phipps, distribution coordinator

PARABOLA ARTS FOUNDATION

656 Broadway
New York, NY 10012-2317
Telephone: (800) 560-MYTH
Fax: (212) 979-7325

Parabola is a society for the study of myth and tradition, and publishes and distributes a quarterly magazine as well as a number of books on traditional worlds of ancient symbol and sacred art, myth and legend, folklore and ritual. It also distributes video and audio programs including *Joseph Campbell and the Power of Myth with Bill Moyers*; *Meetings With Remarkable Men*; *The Mahabharata*; and *A Human Search: The Life of Father Bede Griffiths*.

Year established: 1976

Area(s) of specialty: Print and video works on myth and tradition

Contact: Beth Leonard

KIT PARKER FILMS

P.O. Box 16022
Monterey, CA 93942
Telephone: (408) 393-0303
Fax: (408) 393-0304

Kit Parker Films distributes the classic film libraries of Warner Bros., Orion Pictures, CBS, Republic and various independents in the 35mm theatrical territory. Its agreement with the major studios it represents is a distribution deal; other film deals are negotiated depending upon the picture. Its library includes several thousand classic and contemporary titles. Kit Parker also distributes first-run specialty films for other producers around the world. The company changed its focus over the past few years to theatrical distribution. It screens about 5-6 independent features a week, and estimates that it will distribute one first-run feature per month. Representatives attend AFM, Cannes, and other festivals and markets. Its 1995 release schedule included several reissues and restored features, including *My Fair Lady*; *Clockwork Orange*; *Rebel Without A Cause*; *Cruising*; *Queen of Outer Space*; *In Glorious Black and White*; and *Betty Boop Confidential*; it also included *Arizona Dream* and *Blaxploitation Baby* (a festival of blaxploitation features).

Year established: 1971

Area(s) of specialty: Theatrical distribution of specialty films

Company officers: Kit Parker, president

Number of employees: 10

Contact: Kit Parker

PASSPORT CINEMAS, LTD.

2 Yates Street
Albany, NY 12208
Telephone: (518) 453-1000
Fax: (518) 453-1350

Passport Cinemas is an exhibitor and distributor of independent films, interested in "creating an innovative exhibition and programming network." It considers independent films and videos for non-exclusive distribution to all markets, domestic and international. Passport is looking for shorts, features, documentaries, narrative and experimental productions, which "begin with a worthwhile concept, are well executed, and are well directed—balancing all aspects of the production into an entertaining or interesting whole."

Year established: 1995

Area(s) of specialty: Independent film and video

Company officers: Michael Ellenbogen

Number of employees: 1

Contact: Michael Ellenbogen

PATHE NEWS, INC./PATHE PICTURES, INC.

270 Madison Avenue, 5th floor
New York, NY 10019
Telephone: (212) 696-0392
Fax: (212) 213-5498

Pathe News/Pathe Pictures distributes features, shorts, documentaries, educational and music programs. It has a library of more than 2,000 titles, with 750 in active distribution theatrically, non-theatrically, and to television (public, syndication, and cable) and home video. Some of its titles include *Showtime at the Apollo; Milestones of the Century; Men of Destiny;* as well as a musical library. Distribution is throughout the U.S. as well as Europe, Far East, Australia and Canada; sales agents are used in Great Britain, France, Scandinavia. Representatives attend MIP-TV.

Year established: 1970

Area(s) of specialty: Motion picture and television production and distribution; music library

Number of employees: 6

Company officers: Charles J. Gegen, vice president, Joseph P. Smith, chairman of board, James J. Harrington, secretary, James A. Griffith, treasurer

Contact: Charles J. Gegen, vice president

PBS VIDEO

1320 Braddock Place
Alexandria, VA 22314-1698
Telephone: (703) 739-5000
Fax: (703) 739-0775

PBS Video distributes nearly 800 public television programs throughout the U.S. and Canada, including PBS series programming, documentaries, educational and informational series, dramatic and performing programs, and entertainment specials. It is the exclusive distributor of most of its programs, to non-theatrical and home video markets. The PBS Video library is the largest collection of public television programming in the country, including topics on business, health care, history and social studies, how-to's, humanities, psychology and science. It has a catalog specifically geared to public, school, college and professional libraries, with a variety of pricing options. Many of the programs are packaged as series for wider audience appeal. Its acquisitions are obtained through festivals and submissions to PBS national program series.

Year established: 1977

Area(s) of specialty: PBS accepted programs

Number of employees: 15

Company officers: William T. Reed, senior vice president-PBS Education Services, Jon D. Cecil, director, PBS Video

Contact: Dan Hamby, Associate Director

PHOENIX FILMS AND VIDEO

2349 Chaffee Drive
St. Louis, MO 63146
Telephone: (314) 569-0211
Fax: (314) 569-2834

Phoenix Films, with a library of over 2,000 films and videos, is one of the largest independent educational distributors in the country. It distributes to all markets on a worldwide basis—non-theatrical, semi-theatrical, television, and home video. Its films and videos include shorts, documentary features and shorts, experimental/avant-garde productions, music and arts, animated films, sports, scientific films, and television productions. The catalog includes an extensive array of subjects, including adolescence, advertising, African studies, aging, alcoholism, Americana, animal life, animation, anthropology, architecture, art and art appreciation, art of film, biography and profiles, works by Black filmmakers, career education, child development, Black studies, cities and communities, comparative cultures, dance, earth sciences, economics, English, family life, environmental studies, European studies, fine arts, folktales and fables, foreign language films, future studies, girls' and boys' lives, government, holidays, human relations, humor and satire, literature, motivational films, Native Americans, non-verbal films, photography, philosophy, religion, short stories, values, theater arts, and women filmmakers. It generally acquires productions through submissions from independent producers, and representatives attend Monte Carlo, MIFED, ICEM, IFFM, and AFM. Phoenix is looking for well-made films, particularly 15-30 minute children's films. It may prepare packages or series for greater distribution impact, such as *The Children's Storyteller* and the *Tyler Texas Black Film Collection*. The company has a large sales force, which, in addition to promotional activities such as reviews, new release announcements, special brochures, direct mail and advertising, also conducts workshops and seminars on film utilization.

Year established: 1973
Area(s) of specialty: Educational films to schools and libraries
Company officers: Heinz Gelles, president, Barbara Bryant, vice president,
Bob Dunlap, vice president, sales and marketing
Number of employees: 50
Company officers: Bob Dunlap

PICTURE START, INC.

1727 W. Catalpa Avenue
Chicago, IL 60640-1105
Telephone: (312) 769-2489
Fax: (312) 769-4467

Picture Start specializes in short films and videos, particularly animated, experimental, documentary, dramatic/musical works, and traveling programs of festival winners. Its catalog lists over 750 titles, many of them independent, alternative or unusual productions. It includes works on art and artists, children, comedy/humor/satire, food, death/dying, compilation works, computers, fantasy, language studies, music, dance, portraits/profiles, poetry, nature, theater, women's studies, regional studies, romance, structural/conceptual works. Picture Start's collection is particularly strong in independent animation and short comedy. It will prepare packages or series for greater exposure.

Year established: 1979
Area(s) of specialty: Short films and videos
Contact: Ron Epple

PREMIER STUDIOS

3033 Locust Street
St. Louis, MO 63103
Telephone: (314) 531-3555
Fax: (314) 531-9588

Premier Studios produces and distributes feature films, commercials, educational seminars and music videos. Its target markets, generally, are ad agencies, historical societies, etc.

Year established: 1956
Area(s) of specialty: Film, video and recording
Company officers: Alice Tejada, Sharon Hendrixson, Glenn Hendrixson, Blake Ashby, Tanya Kelley, Dan Thompson
Number of employees: 8-12 full and part time
Contact: Tanya Kelley

PUBLIC MEDIA HOME VIDEO/PUBLIC MEDIA EDUCATION

5547 North Ravenswood Avenue
Chicago, IL 60640-1199
Telephone: (312) 878-2600
Fax: (312) 878-8406

Public Media Incorporated was formed with the purchase of Films Incorporated, a 40-year-old nontheatrical film distribution company, from the Encyclopaedia Britannica Educational Corporation. PMI is the corporate umbrella for Films Incorporated Entertainment, Films Incorporated Quality & Training Resources, and Public Media Education in the nontheatrical market; Public Media Home Video with the Home Vision and Public Media Video labels in the consumer market; PMI Direct, reaching institutional and consumer markets through direct response; and Public Media Television in the broadcast market. The company distributes classic foreign feature films, children's/family programming, fine and performing arts, diverse interests and educational programming. There are over 2,500 works in current distribution, including such titles as *Seven Samurai; The Lion, the Witch, and the Wardrobe; Beauty and the Beast; Civilisation* series; *The Hermitage* series; and *Enter Here*. Acquisitions are selected based on content match to the company's current specialties. Formats also include videodisc, CD-ROM, CCTV, and video on demand.

Year founded: 1968

Area(s) of specialty: Home video, educational media

Company officers: Charles Benton, chairman, Wes Monty, president

Number of employees: 150

Contact: Carole Little

PYRAMID FILM AND VIDEO

2801 Colorado Avenue
Santa Monica, CA 90406
Telephone: (310) 828-7577/(800) 421-2304
Fax: (310) 453-9083

Pyramid Film and Video, with a library of more than 500 titles, distributes films and videos that "educate, inform, inspire and entertain." Its collection contains several types of works: shorts, documentaries, experimental, educational, arts, animated, sports, scientific, television, health, medical, and scientific. A large percentage of its titles come from independent producers. The catalog listings cover over 200 subject areas, including Academy Award nominees and winners, adoption, Africa, affirmative action, archaeology, arts, biography, biology, children's community health education, ecology/ environment, film, folklore, hospital/health care, literature, nonverbal films, new age consciousness, satire, sociology, and women's studies. The company represents established filmmakers as well as student producers. Distribution is to all markets; Pyramid supplies films to over 25,000 film buyers and renters in the U.S. and throughout the world, using sub-distributors in most countries. It also deals directly with end users for special licenses and other distribution. Marketing targets are schools, colleges, universities, libraries, religious groups, non-profit organizations, and health and medical institutions. Films are marketed to free broadcast, non-standard and pay television as well as to other ancillary markets, including stock footage, common carriers, military installations, and consumer video. Its foreign sales representative attends three major markets per year. Contracts are generally exclusive but some are non-exclusive in specific territories or formats. Pyramid enters films in festivals, shows them at conferences and workshops, publicizes them in newsletters and catalogs, and sends them out for reviews. Paid advertising and direct mailing (brochures, posters, special supplements) are utilized. The company also develops film packages for specialized markets such as airlines, college circuits and video networks.

Year established: 1960

Area(s) of specialty: Health, safety, social sciences

Company officers: David Adams, president, Lynn Adams, vice president

Number of employees: 30

Contact: Pat Hamada, director of acquisitions

RAINBOW RELEASING

9165 Sunset Blvd., Suite 300
Los Angeles, CA 90069
Telephone: (310) 271-0202
Fax: (310) 271-2753

Rainbow Releasing looks at "high quality independent films" (35mm feature only) for theatrical distribution. It will look only at completed works for possible distribution (no finishing funds). The company has twelve films in its library, with three in current distribution, including *Last Summer in the Hamptons; Venice/Venice; Love After Love (Après l'Amour); Eating; Babyfever;* and *Mistress.*

Year established: 1970

Area(s) of specialty: Independent films

Company officers: Henry Jaglom, president, Judith Wolinsky, producer, Sharon Lester, distribution

Number of employees: 7

Contact: Sharon Lester

RAVEN PICTURES INTERNATIONAL

859 Hollywood Way, Suite 273
Burbank, CA 91505
Telephone: (818) 508-4785
Fax: (818) 508-4786

Raven Pictures International handles primarily feature films as well as foreign films for worldwide distribution; its sister company, Raven Releasing, focuses on domestic distribution. It acquires small U.S. films which "have strong story and production values" and newly released foreign films available for international and/or U.S. rights. Its goal is two domestic releases per month (theatrical, video and television). Some of the fourteen films currently handled, all in various stages of distribution, are *Extranós Caminos aka Strange Ways; Double Exposure; Stickin' Together;* and *Tie You Up.* Deal structures depend on the individual projects. Submissions from independent filmmakers are welcome. Company representatives attend AFM, Cannes, and MIFED.

Year established: 1994

Area(s) of specialty: Domestic and international feature film distribution

Company officers: Joanne Watkins, president, Scott Wiseman, executive vice president

Number of employees: 8

Contact: Scott Wiseman

REEL MOVIES INTERNATIONAL

8235 Douglas Avenue, Suite 770
Dallas, TX 75225
Telephone: (214) 363-4400
Fax: (214) 739-3456

Reel Movies International specializes in commercial features, documentaries, specialty films, videos and series. It looks for recognizable stars, good scripts and projects in pre-production; action/adventure films and thrillers are the staples of its collection of films. There are over 30 features and over 800 hours of television programming in its library, including such titles as *Cyberstalker; Striking Point; Lethal Betrayal; Timetracers; In a Strange City; Highway to Hell; The Secret; Biotech Warrior; Life of Riley; Takedown; Children of Dracula: Real Interviews with Real Vampires* (documentary); and *The Fearmakers* (series). Distribution of these programs is worldwide theatrically, non-theatrically, to home video and television (public, pay, network, syndication, satellite, and cable). The company can offer some guarantees, and it also has a camera package and lab deals for films that can be shot in Texas. Representatives attend AFM, NATPE, MIP-TV, MIFED, MIPCOM, and MILIA (multimedia).

Year established: 1982

Area(s) of specialty: Foreign distribution

Company officers: Tom T. Moore, president, Dena Moore, contract servicing

Number of employees: 3

Contact: Tom T. Moore

REPUBLIC PICTURES

5700 Wilshire Blvd., #525
Los Angeles, CA 90036
Telephone: (213) 965-6900

Republic Pictures is the production, marketing and distribution arm of
Republic Entertainment, Inc., a unit of Spelling Entertainment, Inc.
Republic/Spelling acquires, produces and distributes independent films.
The company has a library of over 1,400 feature films and 15,000 hours of
television programming. Some of the productions it distributes are *Live
Nude Girls; Black Day Blue Night; Precious Find; Bulletproof Heart;* and *Ruby
in Paradise.*

Area(s) of specialty: Feature film and television distribution

Contact: Tom Szwak, senior vice president, acquisitions

RHAPSODY FILMS, INC.

P.O. Box 179
10 Charlton Street
New York, NY 10014
Telephone: (212) 243-0152
Fax: (212) 645-9250

Rhapsody Films is devoted exclusively to documentary and dramatic films
and videos on music topics, including performances and portraits. Many of
the over 70 titles in its catalog are by independent producers. The catalog
includes such titles as *Texas Tenor: The Illinois Jacquet Story; Colorado
Cowboy: The Bruce Ford Story; Bix: An Interpretation of a Legend; Space is
the Place; Right On! The Roots of Rap; Mingus; Sweet Love; Bitter; Last Date:
Eric Dolphy; The Art Ensemble of Chicago: Live from the Jazz Showcase; Built
by Hand: The String Trio of New York; Land of Look Behind; Heartworm
Highways: The Legends of Country Music's New Wave; Kumu Hula: Keepers
of a Culture;* and *One Hand Don't Clap.* Recent acquisitions include works
on Al Green, Benny Carter, and Sonny Rollins. Schools, colleges, media
centers and libraries account for about a third of the company's sales, video
stores and record chains with video departments account for another third
(e.g., Tower Video, Blockbuster, Borders), and the remainder is mail-order
business domestically and internationally (a major market for its library).
Rhapsody will look at works-in-progress or rough cuts.

Year established: 1982

*Area(s) of specialty: Jazz, blues, world music, modern music, gospel music, country
and western, dramatic and documentary films.*

Company officers: Bruce Ricker, president, Tim Timpanaro, vice-president

Number of employees: 2-3

Contact: Bruce Ricker

RIGEL INDEPENDENT DISTRIBUTION AND ENTERTAINMENT

2338 San Marco Drive
Los Angeles, CA 90068
Telephone: (213) 467-0240
Fax: (213) 467-1679

Rigel Independent Distribution and Entertainment is an international
television and film distribution company which handles the international
distribution of such programs as *RoboCop: The Series*; Buena Vista's *Land's
End*; *Universal Soldier: The Series*; and *Santa Monica Bike Patrol*; and films
such as *The Sadness of Sex* and *Picture Windows*.

Area(s) of specialty: Television and film distribution

Contact: Jim Moyle

RKO PICTURES

1801 Avenue of the Stars
Los Angeles, CA 90067
Telephone: (310) 277-0707
Fax: (310) 284-8574

RKO Pictures is a theatrical film distribution company. Some of the films
it has released include *Last Blossom on the Plum Tree*; *Mata Hari*; *Probable
Cause*; *Beyond a Reasonable Doubt*; *Bedlam*; and *The Locked Room*.

*Company officers: Ted R. Hartley, chairman and CEO, Dina Merrilll, vice-chairman,
Mitch Blumberg, executive vice president*

ROXIE RELEASING

3125 16th Street
San Francisco, CA 94103
Telephone: (415) 431-3611
Fax: (415) 431-2822

Roxie Releasing is related to San Francisco's Roxie Cinema, one of the
longest-running movie theatres in the country. It releases 3-5 films annually. Some of its major successes have included *Red Rock West* and *Vincent*;
other releases include *salmonberries*; *Benny's Video*; *Gimme Shelter* and
Street of No Return. Its interests are foreign films, feature documentaries,
American fiction, and films about writers and artists. The company will
offer advances for U.S. theatrical rights.

Year established: 1985

Area(s) of specialty: Arthouse films

Contact: Bill Banning

SAVOY PICTURES

2425 Olympic Blvd., 6th Floor
Santa Monica, CA 90404
Telephone: (310) 247-7329
Fax: (310) 247-7239

Savoy Pictures, a mini-major, was founded as a distributor of major motion pictures; its releases have included A Bronx Tale; Serial Mom; Exit to Eden; Shadowlands; Last of the Dogmen; The Show; Dr. Jekyll and Ms. Hyde; and Circle of Friends. Recently, it reduced the scale of production, marketing and distribution of feature films, shifting focus to television programming and station acquisitions. The company finances about six films annually, in the $10-20 million range, along with low-budget acquisitions and distribution deals with independents.

Area(s) of specialty: Feature film distribution

Company officers: Victor Kaufman, CEO, Lewis Korman, CEO

Contact: Keven Duffy, creative executive, acquisitions

SELECT MEDIA, INC.

225 Lafayette Street, Suite 1002
New York, NY 10012
Telephone: (212) 431-8923
Fax: (212) 431-8946

Select Media, Inc., distributes educational and documentary videos and CD-ROMs that are "multiculturally based, high-quality, innovative, and curriculum-based." Special emphasis is placed on health and social issue titles. The approximately 75 videos and 50 CD-ROMs in its collection are all in active distribution. Some subject areas covered are HIV/AIDS education, addiction and children, substance-use prevention, family life/self esteem, gender jeopardy, and sexual abuse and domestic violence. Programs include such titles as The AIDSFilms Series; Sex, Drugs & HIV; In Touch: Breast Self-Examination for African-American Teens; Sexual Harassment 101; The Mayo Clinic CD-ROM Health Series; and What is a Bellybutton (CD-ROM). Select Media, Inc., carries videos on an exclusive basis only; CD-ROMs are carried exclusively and non-exclusively. Advances are occasionally offered, but it is rare. The company's primary methods of acquisition are submissions from independent producers, film markets, and known contract producers. Target audiences include schools, libraries, national organizations and associations, governmental agencies, health departments and clinics, colleges and universities. Select Media, Inc., does a great deal of direct-mail marketing, telemarketing and an occasional joint dissemination project with major associations or corporations.

Year established: 1988

Area(s) of specialty: Educational market and non-theatrical market

Company officers: Beth Wachter, president, Helene Fisher, vice president marketing and special projects, Gerson Crespo, distribution manager

Number of employees: 4

Contact: Helene Fisher

SEVENTH ART RELEASING

7551 Sunset Blvd., #104
Los Angeles, CA 90046
Telephone: (213) 845-1455
Fax: (213) 845-4717

Seventh Art Releasing is a full-service North American distribution company which specializes in American independent and foreign features, feature documentaries, and shorts. Some of its releases include *Risk; The Coriolis Effect; Son of the Shark; Sister My Sister; Whale Music;* and *Wall of Silence.*

Year established: 1994

Area(s) of specialty: Feature film distribution

Company officers: Jonathan Cordish, president, Udy Epstein, senior vice president

SHADOW DISTRIBUTION

P.O. Box 1246
Waterville, ME 04903
Telephone: (207) 872-5111
Fax: (207) 872-5502

Shadow Distribution has been running Railroad Square Cinema, Maine's premiere art house cinema, since 1978, and branched out into distribution of feature film. Its titles include *Waterwalker; Latcho Drom;* and *Dance Me Outside.* Shadow hires sub-distributors for all other markets besides theatrical. It utilizes art house cinemas identified through contacts which it developed as a cinema. Representatives attend festivals to look for acquisitions. The company will offer advances, but will not put up production money.

Year established: 1986

Area(s) of specialty: Art house films

Company officers: Ken Eisen, president, Alan Sanborn, vice president

Number of employees: 6 directors/employees

Contact: Ken Eisen, Alan Sanborn

SILVERSTEIN INTERNATIONAL CORPORATION

171 West 57th Street, Suite 12B
New York, NY 10019
Telephone: (212) 541-6620
Fax: (212) 586-0085

Silverstein International Corporation is involved in international distribution, sales, and co-productions. It is "looking to compete more aggressively, through new investments in order to either get involved in new acquisitions, or invest in an exciting new motion picture production." The company "welcomes any type of film" into its catalog. Its current portfolio consists of titles which it represents and others which it owns, including such works as *End of the Game; Blue Sunshine; Blood Beach; The Killing Hour; Dark Places; Left Hand of the Law; Raid on Entebbe; S.H.E.;* and a Warhol-Morrissey Library of 7 films. The company's founder, Maurice "Red" Silverstein has more than 50 years of experience in the film distribution industry. Silverstein handles 6-12 pictures a year, and is involved in financing about 10% of the films it distributes.

Year established: 1970

Area(s) of specialty: Theatrical film distribution

Contact: Eric Silverstein, junior vice president

SONY PICTURES CLASSICS, INC.

550 Madison Avenue
New York, NY 10022
Telephone: (212) 833-8833
Fax: (212) 833-8844

Sony Pictures Classics was formed as an independent New York-based specialized film distribution company in 1992 by the three co-presidents, Michael Barker, Tom Bernard, and Marcie Bloom, who formerly ran Orion Classics and are experts in the area of specialized film acquisition. At Orion, they were responsible for 25% of the 60 most successful specialized films (foreign and low-budget American independent) distributed in the U.S. between 1986 and 1992. Sony Pictures Classics' debut release was *Howard's End*, which grossed over $25 million and won several awards. Sony Pictures Classics has also released *Indochine; The Story of QiuJu; The Long Day Closes; Orlando; Faraway, So Close; L'Accompagnatrice; Belle Epoque; Mi Vida Loca-My Crazy Life; I Don't Want to Talk About It; Vanya on 42nd Street; A Man of No Importance; Martha and Ethel; Farinelli; Burnt by the Sun; Amateur; Crumb; Wings of Courage* (in IMAX 3D); *Love and Human Remains; A Pure Formality; Safe; Living in Oblivion; Mute Witness; Shanghai Triad; The City of Lost Children;* and *Across the Sea of Time*. Acquisitions "is a 365-day-per-year activity," and SPC will consider films from all sources at all stages of completion, looking at works-in-progress and innovative, risky films. SPC generally seeks to acquire North American rights in all media, but can also do deals including international/worldwide territories.

Year established: 1992

Area(s) of specialty: Quality specialized films

Company officers: Michael Barker, co-president, Tom Bernard, co-president, Marcie Bloom, co-president

Number of employees: 15

Contact: Marcie Bloom

STRAND RELEASING

225 Santa Monica Blvd., Suite 810
Santa Monica, CA 90401
Telephone: (310) 395-5002
Fax: (310) 395-2502

Strand Releasing, a distribution as well as a production company, specializes in independent, art, gay, and ethnic films. With over 80 titles in its collection, Strand's films run the gamut from successful theatrical film releases to films geared toward the non-theatrical market. Many of its titles are risky and have been festival award winners. Strand has had considerable theatrical success with art films such as *Crush; All the Vermeers in New York;* and *Faster Pussycat Kill! Kill!;* and gay films such as *Boys Life; For a Lost Soldier;* and *Claire of the Moon.* Generally, Strand will take exclusive rights and decide what it wants to keep, possibly selling off the video and/or cable rights; advances and other deals are decided on a film-by-film basis. Works-in-progress and rough cuts are welcome. Some other titles include *Aileen Wuornos: The Selling of a Serial Killer; Border Radio; Clean, Shaven; Der Elvis; The Golden Boat; The Great Sadness of Zohara; The Hours and Times; Jo-Jo At The Gate of Lions; Noir et Blanc; Macho Dancer; Magdalena Viraga; My Degeneration; The Natural History of Parking Lots; Surviving Desire; Postcards From America; Roy Cohn/Jack Smith; Terminal U.S.A; Three Bewildered People In The Night; Totally F***ed Up; Twister;* and *Wild Reeds.*

Year established: 1989

Area(s) of specialty: Art films, theatrical releases

Company officers: Marcus Hu, co-president, Jon Gerrans, co-president, Mike Thomas, co-president

Number of employees: 6

Contact: Marcus Hu, Monica Bider

SUNBURST COMMUNICATIONS, INC.

39 Washington Avenue
Pleasantville, NY 10570
Telephone: (914) 769-5030/(800) 431-1934
Fax: (914) 769-5211

Sunburst Communications distributes videos and print materials for grades 2–12 in areas such as drug education, health, guidance, careers and family life. The company sells to schools, institutions and agencies in North America.

Area(s) of specialty: Educational media

Contact: Susan Green

SWANK MOTION PICTURES

350 Vanderbilt Motor Parkway
Hauppauge, NY 11781-4305
Telephone: (516) 434-1560
Fax: (516) 434-1574
910 Riverside Drive
Elmhurst, IL 60126-4967
Telephone: (708) 833-0061
Fax: (708) 833-0096
201 S. Jefferson Avenue
St. Louis, MO 63103-2579
Telephone: (314) 534-6300
Fax: (314) 289-2192

Swank Motion Pictures is a distribution source company handling licensing of classic and new releases from major Hollywood studios, including United Artists, Warner Brothers, MGM, Walt Disney, Universal, Gramercy, Orion, Hollywood Pictures, Turner Home Entertainment, Miramax and Touchstone Pictures. The company handles non-theatrical exhibition for films available in 35mm, 16mm, and public performance video, with several hundred titles listed in its catalog.

Area(s) of specialty: Theatrical films

Contact: Swank programmer

TAPESTRY INTERNATIONAL, LTD.

920 Broadway, Suite 1501
New York, NY 10010
Telephone: (212) 505-2288
Fax: (212) 505-5059

Tapestry International is a New York City-based foreign and domestic distribution company which is a force in the supply of independently produced quality programming to the worldwide marketplace. Initially established in 1982 as a production and post-production facility, it expanded in 1987 to include international distribution. With its recent acquisition of Public Television International (PTI), Tapestry has a diverse collection of over 500 films. It sells worldwide through its attendance at the major television markets MIP-TV, MIPCOM, Monte Carlo, NATPE, Sunny Side of the Doc and MIP-Asia, exhibiting at each of these venues with pre-arranged screenings with hundreds of buyers. The company also participates in film festivals and the IFP market. Its library includes several award-winning dramas, performance arts and entertainment/music, children's, cultural, narrative and documentary programming. Actively involved in co-productions, the company works with major world broadcasters on new projects. Tapestry-distributed programs have been sold to television in Australia, Canada, Ireland, Sweden, Japan, Germany, France, Spain, the U.K., Asia, Eastern Europe, Seoul and the Middle East. Titles in the catalog include numerous independently produced programs such as *The Need For Speed; Dream Deceivers; NOVA; The American Experience; Death In Venice-CA; The Second Greatest Story Ever Told; Legends In Light; If The Mango Tree Could Speak; The Obit Writer; Kalamazoo; Bond & Donnel;* and selected titles from *Great Performances* such as *The World of Jim Henson.*

Year established: 1987

Area(s) of specialty: Broadcast, cable and home video markets.

Company officers: Nancy Walzog, president, Myriam Duteil, director of sales

Number of employees: 30

Contact: Anthony LaTorella, acquisitions

TAPEWORM VIDEO DISTRIBUTORS

12420 Montague Street
Arleta, CA 91331
Telephone: (818) 896-8899
Fax: (818) 896-3855

Tapeworm Video Distributors specializes in domestic video acquisition and distribution of unusual films, including foreign films, independent American releases and avant-garde productions.

Area(s) of specialty: Video rentals

TARA RELEASING

124 Belvedere Street
San Rafael, CA 94901-4707
Telephone: (415) 454-5838

Some 1995 releases included *Colorado Cowboy: The Bruce Ford Story; Freedom on My Mind; High Lonesome; The Secret Adventures of Tom Thumb; Toward the Within: Dead Can Dance;* and *Wings of Honneamise.* The company hires in-house publicists to get the word out and guide marketing efforts.

Company officers: Guy Cables

TAURUS ENTERTAINMENT COMPANY

Sunset Gower Studios
1420 N. Beachwood Drive
Box 2, Bldg. 50
Hollywood, CA 90028
Telephone: (213) 993-7355
Fax: (213) 993-7316

Taurus Entertainment looks for features and commercially viable productions. There are about 45 titles in its collection, with 30 in current distribution, including such titles as *Kentucky Fried Movie, CA;* and *Compromising Positions.* The company distributes to all media.

Year established: 1987
Area(s) of specialty: Commercial properties
Company officers: Stanley Dudelson, Jim Dudelson, Robert Dudelson
Number of employees: 6
Contact: Mona Massof

CHIP TAYLOR COMMUNICATIONS

15 Spollett Drive
Derry, NH 03038
Telephone: (603) 434-9262
Fax: (603) 434-9262
e-mail: chiptaylor@delphi.com

Chip Taylor Communications distributes to the educational non-theatrical market, as well as to television, home video and semi-theatrical outlets, including schools, colleges, libraries, organizations and businesses. Its library currently contains a wide range of 700 titles, including features, shorts, documentary, animated, sports, educational, and experimental programs. Works on reading (language arts/children's literature, storytelling/ legends and folklore), English (writers and poetry, contemporary literature/ creative writing), social studies (contemporary world studies/geography/ travel, world cultures, contemporary world events, sociology, women's studies, world history, U.S. history, U.S. government/civics, U.S. multi-culture studies), science, mathematics, computer science, physical education (fitness/wellness, recreation/self-defense/sports/sports safety), health (guidance, AIDS and substance abuse, parenting/childbirth, medicine, aging/the elderly), arts (performing arts, animation, studio and visual arts, art appreciation, architecture), vocational education, staff development, special education, and special interest are included. The company prefers series of titles; educational titles should be curriculum-oriented, and special-interest films and videos should be on contemporary subject matter. Producers should send a VHS copy of the film or video with a SASE. The company will provide some advances and guarantees, and will look at works-in-progress and rough cuts. The bulk of the company's sales are to non-theatrical and home video markets; another 10% is theatrical and semi-theatrical. The bulk of television sales (70%) are to public and cable television. Special marketing tools include e-mail, special interest magazines, special interest stores, and cable television.

Year established: 1985
Area(s) of specialty: Educational, documentaries, special interest videos
Company officers: Chip Taylor, president
Number of employees: 1
Contact: Chip Taylor

THIRD WORLD NEWSREEL

335 West 38th Street, 5th Floor
New York, NY 10018
Telephone: (212) 947-9277
Fax: (212) 594-6417

For over 25 years, Third World Newsreel, one of the oldest Third World media centers in the country, has been producing and distributing films and videos by and about people of color in the U.S., and by Third World peoples throughout the world. It was one of the first independent media groups to document progressive movements which were generally ignored by the mass media. Newsreel has produced dozens of documentaries on the anti-Vietnam war effort, the civil rights and the Black Power movement, the Puerto Rican Young Lords, the womens' movement, and liberation movements throughout the world. It continues to produce, distribute and exhibit social issue documentaries and experimental and alternative media, with over 200 films and videos from the African, Asian, Latina/o, Arab and Native American diasporas. Its collection includes works by award winning film and video artists such as Charles Burnett, Julie Dash, Camille Billops, Guillermo Gomez Peña, Shu Lea Cheang, Gurinder Chadha, Isaac Julien, Michelle Parkerson, Roddy Bogawa, Tania Cypriano, Thomas Allen Harris, and Maureen Blackwood. Third World Newsreel also sponsor on-going touring exhibition projects, offering film and video packages from developing nations and communities. Past touring exhibitions have included "Internal Exile: New Films and Videos from Chile," "D'Ghetto Eyes: New Works by Emerging Black, Asian, Latina/o and Native Video Makers," "Liberation and Alienation in Algerian Cinema," and "Look at My People: The El Salvadoran Revolution," by the El Salvador Media Project. The organization's catalog includes films and videos in such categories as "Voices from the African Diaspora," "Re-Imagining the 'Orient': Videos from the Middle East," "First Peoples' Visions," "The Asian Diaspora," and "Cross Cultural Perspectives." General target audiences include colleges, high schools, libraries, museums, community and student groups, activists and artists.

Year established: 1967
Area(s) of specialty: Works by makers of color and Third World social issues
Company officers: Ada Gay Griffin
Number of employees: 6
Contact: Ada Gay Griffin

TRANSCONTINENTAL PICTURES INDUSTRIES

650 North Bronson Avenue
Hollywood, CA 90004
Telephone: (213) 464-2279
Fax: (213) 464-3212

Transcontinental Pictures Industries distributes action, adventure, science fiction, dramatic, comedy and family films worldwide. It will handle any film "well acted, well directed and well produced." Some of the titles it has distributed include A Man Called Intrepid; Code Name Zebra; Another Time Another Place; and Grandpa. It will look at works-in-progress or rough cuts (the company's policy), and can offer advances.

Year established: 1969

Area(s) of specialty: All media worldwide

Company officers: Israel Shaked, president, Robert Kilgore, vice president-acquisitions

Number of employees: 3

Contact: Robert Kilgore

TRIDENT RELEASING

8401 Melrose Place, 2nd Floor
Los Angeles, CA 90069
Telephone: (213) 655-8818
Fax: (213) 655-0515

Trident Releasing distributes feature films, and is looking for films which are low budget but have good production values, acting and storylines. The company acquires all types of films for the international market (its most important). Representatives attend all major markets, including Cannes, MIFED and AFM. Some of its current titles include $E=MC^2$; Point of Betrayal; The Last Fair Deal; The Little Patriot; Back Fire!; and Solitaire for 2. It accepts submissions from independent producers; individual distribution deals are negotiated depending upon the picture.

Year established: 1989

Area(s) of specialty: Feature films

Company officers: Jean Ovrum, Victoria Plummer

Number of employees: 6

Contact: Barbara Mannion

TRIMARK PICTURES

2644 30th Street
Santa Monica, CA 90405
Telephone: (310) 314-2000
Fax: (310) 452-9614

Trimark Pictures is a broad-based producer and distributor of feature films, distributing 8-10 films theatrically annually and 45 films to the home video market. Some of its releases include Separate Lives; Federal Hill; Swimming With Sharks; and Kicking and Screaming.

Area(s) of specialty: Feature film production and distribution

Contact: Bobby Rock, director of acquisitions

TRIUMPH FILMS

10202 West Washington Blvd.
Culver City, CA 90232
Telephone: (310) 280-4036
Fax: (310) 280-4988

Triumph Films is Sony Pictures lower-budget production and acquisition arm. Its films are released worldwide through Columbia/TriStar. Some of its releases are *Jury Duty*; *Screamers*; and *Nina Takes a Lover*.

Area(s) of specialty: Feature film distribution

Contact: Jean-Luc de Fanti, director of acquisitions

TROMA, INC.

1501 Broadway #2605
New York, NY 10036
Telephone: (212) 997-0595
Fax: (212) 997-0968

Troma, Inc. produces, acquires and distributes low-budget action/horror/mystery commercial exploitation films aimed at young adult audiences. It now has a library of 70 features, distributed to all worldwide markets, including theatrical, cable, television and home video. The company has an exclusive agent for Japan, and handles all other territories itself through its in-house international sales department. Representatives attend Cannes, AFM, MIFED, IFP, MIPCOM, Tokyo, Toronto, MystFest and others. Some of its titles are *The Toxic Avenger (Parts I, II, and III)*; *Stuff Stephanie in the Incinerator*; *Fortress of Amerikkka*; *Troma's War*; *Monster in the Closet*; *The Class of Nuke 'Em High*; *Student Confidential*; and *Surf Nazis Must Die*. Troma creates slicks, posters, contests, and give-aways (t-shirts, Troma perfume, etc.). All advertising is done by its subsidiary TRC Advertising.

Year established: 1974

Area of specialty (s): Film production and distribution

Number of employees: 20

Company officers: Lloyd Kaufman, president, Michael Herz, vice president/Ron Goldberg, Director of Acquisitions

Contact: Ron Goldberg/Carl Morano

UNITED LEARNING, INC.

6633 West Howard Street
Niles, IL 60648
Telephone: (708) 647-0600
Fax: (708) 647-0918

United Learning distributes curriculum-correlated educational instructional materials that are generally video based and geared to all grade levels

(K-12): science, math, language arts, social studies, guidance and coun-seling, and other curriculum-related areas. Its markets include public and private schools and public libraries, with sales agents used in Canada, Australia, United Kingdom, Taiwan, and Malaysia. Most programs are dis-tributed on a royalty basis, and the company works with independent and contract producers. New producers are frequently handled "as long as their production quality meets broadcast standards." There are over 350 titles in its collection, which is growing through a combination of telemarketing, direct mail, catalogs, exhibits at major educational conferences, advertising in trade journals, and a dealer network of over 100 sub-distributors.

Year established: 1969

Area(s) of specialty: Curriculum based educational videos

Company officers: Ronald E. Reed, president, Frank Marquett, treasurer

Number of employees: 32

Contact: Ronald E. Reed

UNITED NATIONS AUDIO VISUAL PROMOTION AND DISTRIBUTION

Dept. of Public Information, Media Division, Room S-805A
United Nations
New York, NY 10017
Telephone: (212) 963-6982
Fax: (212) 963-6869
e-mail: sue-ting-len@un.org.

The United Nations distributes over 120 television and video programs on numerous international issues. Distribution is worldwide to broadcasters, satcasters, cable stations, theatrical, non-theatrical, home video, educa-tional, governmental and non-governmental users. The programs in its library include documentary features and shorts, educational, animation and television series. Target audiences are all age groups, through the U.N.'s Information Centers. The U.N. Department of Public Information maintains 130 regional libraries in its Information Centres and United Nations Development Programme offices throughout the world, serviced from U.N. Headquarters in New York. The regional libraries offer a wide selection of U.N. films for loan to broadcasters, educational institutions and non-governmental organizations. In several of these libraries, there are regular screenings of U.N. films and videos. Additionally, the U.N. grants sales and rental rights to distributors worldwide.

Year established: 1945

Area(s) of specialty: International issues, documentaries

Contact: Barbara Sue-Ting-Len

UNIVERSITY OF CALIFORNIA EXTENSION CENTER FOR MEDIA AND INDEPENDENT LEARNING

2000 Center Street, 4th Floor
Berkeley, CA 94704
Telephone: (510) 642-0460
Fax: (510) 643-9271
e-mail: dbickley@uclink.berkeley.edu

Formerly the Extension Media Center, the Center for Media and Independent learning is the worldwide media distribution agency for the University of California. It represents independent producers from throughout the country and the world, focusing on high quality documentaries and creative educational productions, and offering royalties based on a negotiated percentage of gross revenues. Exclusive rights are needed for the educational market but are not insisted on for other markets. Each year CMIL releases 25-40 new titles, and maintains a collection of about 500 films and videos. New acquisitions are selected on the basis of their "educational merit and significance, production quality, originality and sales potential." CMIL distributes documentaries and educational productions to colleges, universities, and scholarly institutions around the world (about 60% of sales), health and mental health facilities and agencies (about 20% of sales), and K-12 public and private schools (about 20% of sales), as well as to cable and broadcast television, museums, public libraries, home video and businesses. It has sales representatives throughout much of the U.S. and subdistributors and agents in Canada, Australia, Italy, Spain, and Asia. Marketing strategies are developed for each title, emphasizing brochures and flyers sent to highly targeted mailing lists, publicity campaigns, reviews, entry into conferences and festivals, and occasional paid ads. New titles are featured prominently in the catalog, and numerous subject-area brochures are mailed each year; some older titles are typically promoted over many years. The programs CMIL distributes cover a wide range of subjects, including anthropology and ethnography, social and clinical psychology and psychotherapy, American history, multicultural and ethnic studies, women's studies, social issues, environment, animal behavior, science, arts, religion, health and medical sciences, and educational issues. CMIL will look at personal and artistic works if they have potential for educational sales. Representatives attend a variety of conferences and festivals. Some examples of titles are *Ishi, The Last Yahi; Forever Activists: The Story of the Veterans of the Abraham Lincoln Brigade; In and Out of Africa.*

Year established: 1916

Area(s) of specialty: Educational media

Company officers: Daniel Bickley, media marketing, Mary Beth Almed, director

Number of employees: 15

Contact: Daniel Bickley

UPSTATE FILMS

P.O. Box 324
Rhinebeck, NY 12572
Telephone: (914) 876-4546
Fax: (914) 876-2353

Upstate Films has been programming independent films at its arthouse in Rhinebeck for over two decades. Its new distribution company, in partnership with International Film Circuit, is interested in well-done, off-beat films which have done well on the festival circuit. It has released *Anchoress* as its first film. The company hopes to book films into calendar houses and art houses in major markets.

Area(s) of specialty: Independent film distribution and exhibition
Contact: Steve Leiber

VIDEO DATA BANK

School of the Art Institute of Chicago
37 S. Wabash
Chicago, IL 60603
Telephone: (312) 345-3550
Fax: (312) 541-8073

Video Data Bank, a non-profit distributor, is one of the largest distributors of videos by and about contemporary artists in the country, with 3,000 titles in its archive and 1,200 in distribution. These works cover art and politics, feminist issues, Latin American issues, performance, sculpture and painting, experimental video art, gender and sexuality, media and media criticism, photography and photo criticism, and video history. Video Data Bank-distributed tapes are used each year by hundreds of arts, educational, broadcast, and community-based organizations; it "offers innovative work that challenges the conventions of the television medium, while speaking about personal experience, political ideas, and the diverse fabric of modern culture." The company is looking for experimental video art dealing with contemporary ideas and issues as well as documentaries on contemporary artists, including performance. It acquires about 50 videos annually, and has employed several aggressive marketing strategies and innovative special projects to keep pace with the expansion of the video field, including expansion into foreign markets (Europe, Latin America, Japan and Australia) and growth in the U.S., including community-based organizations. Overseas, it has non-formal arrangements with European distributors, and representatives attend European markets and festivals to promote the work in its collection. Video Data Bank also enters programs into several international film/video festivals. Contracts are non-exclusive. It purchases mailing lists for specific titles and develops promotional brochures, as well as direct mailings, postcards and personal phone contact with clients. It also provides a complete selection of materials with the videos it offers, including program

notes, photos, slides, videographies and biographies. Several of Video
Data Bank's works are grouped in special collections. These include the
Independent Video/Alternative Media Collection, which includes over 1,000
recent titles by approximately 200 independent producers, collectives, and
artists, and features work on topics such as activist and guerrilla television,
sexuality, feminism, media criticism, censorship, the multicultural experience, history, the environment, formal innovations, civil liberties, AIDS,
reproductive rights, and health care; *Early U.S. Video Art*, with seminal
works from video's formative period beginning in 1968, including the historic Castelli-Sonnabend Collection and the guerrilla works of Top Value
Television and Ant Farm; and *On Art and Artists*, a collection of over 250
tapes featuring interviews with contemporary critics, composers, painters,
photographers and sculptors and in-depth documentaries on artists. Other
special projects include *Video Drive In*, a free outdoor event designed to
draw very large public audiences (5,000-10,000 per screening), and which
has been presented in Barcelona, Valencia, Lisbon, New York, and Chicago;
and the *Home Library Series*, including *Video Against AIDS* and *What Does
She Want*, a compilation of leading work in film, performance and video by
women addressing the themes of feminism. Video Data Bank can offer
compilation services for nominal rates.

Year established: 1976

*Area(s) of specialty: Experimental video, AIDS activism work, documentaries on
contemporary artists.*

Company officers: Kate Horsfield, director, Mindy Faber, associate director

Number of employees: 7

Contact: Ayanna Udongo, director of outreach

VIDEODISC PUBLISHING, INC./VPI/AC VIDEO, INC.

381 Park Ave South, Suite 620
New York, NY 10016
Telephone: (212) 685-5522
Fax: (212) 685-5482

Videodisc Publishing distributes cultural, travel and art titles (including
museums and artists), many submitted by independent producers, to home
video, catalogs and educational markets.

Year established: 1983

Formats Handled: 1/2" (VHS), Videodisc (CAV, CLV)

Area(s) of specialty: Culture, art, travel

Number of employees: 4

Company officer: Gene Fairly

Contact: Gary Beharry

THE VIDEO PROJECT

5332 College Avenue, Suite 101
Oakland, CA 94168
Telephone: (415) 655-9050
Fax: (415) 655-9115

The Video Project (films and videos for a safe and sustainable world) is a non-profit distributor which specializes in documentary and educational programs, including video releases and multimedia programs, about the environment (ancient forests/ancient peoples, protecting natural resources, water, wildlife, food and agriculture, the atmosphere, waste and toxics, ethics and values, sustainable development, energy and transportation), human rights (rights and wrongs, Latin America, Former Soviet Union, Eastern Europe), nuclear (nuclear energy, Hiroshima/Nagasaki, nuclear testing, nuclear legacy, nuclear waste, nuclear proliferation) and war and peace issues (domestic impact, wounds of war, Gulf war). It looks for "engaging styles provoking thought and discussion." Its catalog includes over 250 titles on a wide range of subjects, including several recent Oscar winners and nominees, as well as many programs that have received top awards at major film festivals and recommendations from key review publications. The library includes The Video Project's own productions as well as submissions from independent producers. Some titles include *The Mighty River*; *Eco-Rap: Voices From the Hood*; *Deadly Deception*; *Battle for the Trees*; *Return of the Scorcher*; *The Man Who Planted Trees*; *Toxic Racism*; *Rights and Wrongs*; *Ghosts Along the Freeway*; *The Heartbeat of America*; *Sadako and the Thousand Paper Cranes*; *Building Bombs: The Legacy*; *Dark Circle*; *When the Spill Hit Homer*; and *The Panama Deception*. The main distribution focus is to home video and institutions, universities, secondary schools, and grassroots groups. It has used both independent publicists and in-house marketing specialists, and direct mail utilizing its existing database and purchase of lists, to market its films and videos. The largest audience is K-12 and college.

Year established: 1983

Area(s) of specialty: Documentaries about environment, human rights, nuclear and peace issues

Company officers: Steve Ladd, executive director, Ian Thiermann, treasurer, Vivienne Verdon-Roe, president

Number of employees: 5

Contact: Steve Ladd

VISION MAKERS VIDEO

Native American Public Broadcasting Consortium
P.O. Box 83111
Lincoln, NE 68501
Telephone: (402) 472-3522
Fax: (402) 472-8675

The Native American Public Broadcasting Consortium, established in 1977, has "the responsibility of bringing the voices and faces of Native America to the Public Broadcasting System." Its mandate is "to inform, educate, and encourage the awareness of tribal histories, cultures, languages, opportunities, and aspirations through the fullest participation of American Indians and Alaska Natives in creating and employing all forms of educational and public telecommunications programs and services, thereby supporting tribal sovereignty." As a member of the National Minority Consortia, it solicits program development grants for independent and station-based Native American programs. Its Vision Makers Video subsidiary focuses on documentary/educational videos about Native Americans which are accurate portrayals of Native American culture. Its catalog lists 182 titles, of which 178 are actively distributed. Some of its titles are *American Indian Artist* series; *Forest Spirits* series; *Images of Indians* series; *Indian Arts at the Phoenix Heard Museum* series; *Ni'bthaska of the Umonhon* series; *People of the First Light* series; *Destiny Uncertain* series; *The Real People* series; *Tales of the Wesakechak* series; *We Are One* series; *Winds of Change* series; *Indians of North America* series; *Marks of the Ancestors*; *The Beginning of a New Life*.

Company officers: Frank Blythe, executive director

Number of employees: 6

Year established: 1977

Area of specialty: Public television programs and educational video distribution

Contact: Matthew L. Jones, sales and acquisitions specialist

VISION VIDEO/GATEWAY FILMS, INC.

P.O. Box 540
2030 Wentz Church Road
Worcester, PA 19490
Telephone: (215) 584-1893
Fax: (215) 584-4610
e-mail: visionvide@aol.com

Vision Video/Gateway Films, Inc., distributes films to non-theatrical, home video and television markets, with a concentration of its titles in religion, history and social issues. It has about 250 titles in its collection. The company uses sub-distributors in over 50 cities and sales agents in U.K., Europe, Australia, New Zealand, Philippines, and Hong Kong; promotional activities include reviews, press releases, convention booths, heavy direct-mail concentration, promotions sent to sub-distributors. Representatives attend MIP and AFM. Target audiences include schools, churches, individual consumers (home video), television, and libraries.

Year established: 1981

Area(s) of specialty: Religion, history

Company officers: A. Kenneth Curtis, William Curtis

Contact: William Curtis

VISTA STREET ENTERTAINMENT

9911 West Pico Blvd., Suite PH-P
Los Angeles, CA 90035
Telephone: (310) 556-3074
Fax: (310) 556-8815

With about 30 films in its catalog, Vista Street Entertainment specializes in international sales and handles feature releases to the home video and pay and cable markets; the company develops and produces its own material. It looks for works of good quality both in subject matter and technical approach, with a commercial edge. Representatives attend Cannes, IFFM, AFM, and MIFED. Some titles released by Vista Street Entertainment, which include witchcraft, erotic thriller, adventure, action, comedy and drama, include *Dark Angel; Salem's Ghost; Sweet Evil; Street Vengeance; Flight to Danger; Narcotic Justice; The Temptress; The Virgin Heart; Dance with the Devil; A Taste For Blood; Body Parts;* and *Cybernator*.

Year established: 1977

Area(s) of specialty: Erotic thrillers, action films

Company officers: Gerald Feifer, president, Michael Feifer, vice president, production and interactive, Alexander Witlin, vice president international distribution

Number of employees: 3

Contact: Gerald Feifer

VOCATIONAL MARKETING SERVICES (VMS)

17600 South Williams Street, #6
Thornton, IL 60476
Telephone: (708) 877-2814
Fax: (708) 877-2819

Vocational Marketing Services is a video distributor specializing in vocational education, industrial training materials, home economics, trade and industrial, career and guidance, business and technical subjects. Its primary markets are schools and industry. With over 2,000 titles in its library, it expands its collection through catalogs, trade shows, and referrals. The titles come from 200 publisher/producers, including Taunton Press, Hometime, New Yankee Workshop, Champion Auto and Intertec. Its training videos cover such areas of instruction as computer use, cabinetmaking, and homebuilding. Vocational Marketing Services produces five catalogs and attends over fifty shows annually. Many of its clients are industrial companies which produced a training video for internal use and found that it could sell it for them at a profit.

Year established: 1986

Area(s) of specialty: Vocational education

Company officers: Michael S. Walsh, president, Lydia Walsh, head buyer

Number of employees: 9

Contact: Michael S. Walsh, Lydia Walsh

WARNER HOME VIDEO

4000 Warner Blvd.
Burbank, CA 91522
Telephone: (818) 954-6000
Fax: (818) 954-6540

Warner Home Video has an extensive library of over 1000 titles for sale in
its domestic catalog, with programs ranging from major commercial theatrical features to special interest video to children's programming. Its catalog
lists new releases, its current library, family entertainment, documentary
and special interest, general library works on video. Warner distributes
throughout North America and internationally. Extensive publicity activities include public relations mailings, sales promotion aids, in-store POP,
dealer preview reels, servicing of clip reels to broadcast media, television
and radio advertising, selected print media, etc. Representatives attend all
of the major film markets.

Area(s) of specialty: Entertainment programming

Contact: Vice president, acquisitions, worldwide

WOMEN MAKE MOVIES

462 Broadway
New York, NY 10013
Telephone: (212) 925-0606
Fax: (212) 925-2052

Women Make Movies is a national, non-profit feminist media center dedicated to the production, promotion and distribution of films and videos by
and about women. It is a multicultural, multiracial organization which also
provides a number of services to independent producers in addition to distribution, including publications (including a Women of Color Database),
technical assistance (fiscal sponsorship, a resource center, screening room,
skills bank, and a production division) and training programs (including
production of a limited number of films and videos). It "remains dedicated
to changing the representation of women in the media by promoting a
diversity of styles, subjects and perspectives in women's media." Women
Make Movies is the leading distributor in the U.S. of films and videos by
women, with a diverse collection of more than 400 theatrical features,
experimental short films, documentaries, and video art. Its catalog of films
and videos lists works by women on such topics as sex equity, health, gender, global perspectives and cultural identity, and arts. Women Make Movies
is interested in handling extremely risky films, both in form and in content;
its first concern is quality, not commercial concerns. Distribution is to all
markets—theatrical, nontheatrical, semi-theatrical, television (public, pay,
satellite, and cable). Contracts are exclusive, except under special circumstances and for video art. Extensive promotional activity includes sending
tapes to major reviewers, festivals, and programmers, printing specialty
brochures on collections of films/tapes, production of one-sheets, and some

paid advertising; packages may also be prepared. Women Make Movies is a domestic distributor but will distribute to all territories (including Asia, Africa, Europe and Latin America) if a producer does not have foreign distributors. Representatives attend the most important international festivals for acquisitions, including Toronto, Berlin, Montreal, as well as smaller festivals and women's festivals. Some new acquisitions in 1995 included *All Fall Down; Brincando El Charco; Coconut/Cane & Cutlass; Columbus on Trial; Complaints of a Dutiful Daughter; Daughters of Dykes; Dialogues with Madwomen; Dream Girls; Greetings From Africa; Home Away From Home; Iraqi Women; Las Madres; Long Time Comin'; The Mother; No Means No; Not Just Passing Through; On Cannibalism; Outlaw; Praise House; Ripples of Change; Saar; Tanto Tiempo; The Trained Chinese Tongue; Which Way is East; Who's Going to Pay for These Donuts, Anyway?; A Woman Waiting for Her Period; Women of Niger;* and *Yuri Kochiyama.*

Year established: 1972

Area(s) of specialty: Film and video works by women about women

Company officers: Debra Zimmerman, executive director, Sasha Berman, distribution operations manager, Claudette Furlonge, administrative manager, Terry Lawler, director of development and production, Jennifer Stott, director of sales and promotion, Dorothy Thigpen, director of membership and production services

Number of employees: 8 full-time, 5 part-time

Contact: Debra Zimmerman

WORLD WIDE PICTURES, INC.

1201 Hennepin Avenue
Minneapolis, MN 55459
Telephone: (612) 338-3335
Fax: (612) 338-3029

World Wide Pictures distributes Christian and evangelistic films, with about 75-100 works in its library. Distribution is international, to theatrical, television and home video markets.

Year established: 1951

Area(s) of specialty: Christian full-length films

Number of employees: 33

Contact: Barry Werner

ZEITGEIST FILMS, LTD.

247 Centre Street, 2nd Floor
New York, NY 10013
Telephone: (212) 274-1989
Fax: (212) 274-1644
e-mail: zeitgeist@tunanet.com

Zeitgeist Films, Ltd., is a distributor of independent features and documentaries. It takes on five films per year that need special marketing or handling, and "gives them the best and most effective distribution in all markets." Distribution encompasses theatrical, semi-theatrical, and non-theatrical markets. Zeitgeist also handles television and home video sales, which includes laserdisc and other new technologies. Its catalog contains around fifty titles covering such areas as AIDS, animation, Asian Studies, Black Studies, British film, Canadian film, comedy, documentaries, Eastern European cinema, East Germany, family, gay and lesbian, history, politics, sex roles, Tibet and women's studies. Zeitgeist recently released *1-900; Art for Teachers of Children; Ballot Measure Nine;* and *Dottie Gets Spanked.* Other titles include *Faust; Manufacturing Consent: Noam Chomsky and the Media; Coming Out Under Fire; The Forbidden Quest; Silverlake Life: The View From Here; Poison; Lightning Over Braddock; Vermont is for Lovers; Painting the Town;* and *London;* as well as films by Bruce Weber, Yvonne Rainer, Derek Jarman, Guy Maddin, Atom Egoyan, Peter Greenaway, the Brothers Quay, and Apparatus.

Year established: 1988

Area(s) of specialty: Independent features and documentaries

Company officers: Nancy Gerstman, co-president, Emily Russo, co-president

Number of employees: 2

Contact: Nancy Gerstman, Emily Russo

ZENGER MEDIA

10,200 Jefferson Blvd.
Culver City, CA 90232
Telephone: (310) 839-2436/(800) 421-4246

Zenger Media distributes a wide variety of supplementary curriculum materials, including videos, to schools with a strong emphasis on history, government and current affairs.

Area(s) of specialty: Social studies school service

Contact: Manager

STRATEGY AND TACTICS IN ORCHESTRATING THE DISTRIBUTION DEAL

Mark Litwak

hen a distributor negotiates with a filmmaker to acquire film rights, the distributor often has a lot of clout and the filmmaker may be desperate to make a deal. This is a perilous situation for the filmmaker. A filmmaker who makes a bad distribution deal will not be able to repay investors, and this often means the filmmaker will find it very difficult, if not impossible, to make another independent film. Filmmakers must know how to orchestrate the release of their film into the marketplace so that the filmmaker is at his/her competitive best when it comes time to negotiate the distribution deal.

Unfortunately, making the film is only half the battle. In order to secure favorable terms for distribution, a filmmaker needs to have a strategy designed to attract distributors to the film. This often entails generating good word-of-mouth within the industry. This "buzz" or "heat" can be encouraged by filmmakers who are willing to work the festival circuit and mount a campaign on behalf of the film.

Festivals are a cost-effective way to get films in front of potential distributors. Acquisition executives tend to attend some festivals more than others. They prefer to attend festivals that premiere films with distribution rights still available. Festivals compete with each other in order to premiere such films. They each want to be first to discover a great film. Filmmakers need to understand that you only get one premiere per territory or region, and participation in one festival may make the film ineligible for other festivals. For instance, the Sundance Film Festival has a policy of only accepting films that have been in one festival before Sundance. Note that Sundance does not count markets, such as AFM and IFFM, as a festival.

The festivals most important for filmmakers seeking distribution are those that are well attended by acquisition executives. There are many festivals and they each have their own selection criteria and point of view. Some are specialized; others exhibit a broad range of motion pictures including animation, shorts and documentaries. The nature of a film will determine which festivals are best to enter. Generally speaking, for independent filmmakers with feature-length films, the best festivals and markets are The Independent Feature Film Market (IFFM), Sundance, Hamptons International Film Festival, New York and Telluride. The most important international festivals and markets are Berlin, Cannes, Toronto, and Venice.

When you attend a festival come early and bring lots of marketing materials. Some filmmakers show up the day of their screening and don't understand why only a handful of acquisition executives have attended their screening and the distribution offers are not pouring in. Other wiser filmmakers spend a considerable amount of time laying the groundwork for a successful festival. They prepare professional one-sheets (8.5 x 11" handouts that look like little film posters), posters, T-shirts and giveaway items. Sometimes they arrange publicity stunts to call attention to their films. Often it is useful to have the stars attend the festival.

In 1994 I attended the IFFM representing the film *Unconditional Love*. I met with the filmmaker and his collaborators beforehand and we plotted a strategy. The film is an autobiographical account of a young painter searching for his artistic vision amid his various romantic entanglements. It is a classy art film. We devised a professional full-color glossy one-sheet with still photos from the film, a beautiful poster and a press kit with photos, a synopsis, bios and other information about the film. We also decided to produce a unique giveaway: a small artist's sketch pad with the film's artwork and screening times on the cover. This giveaway was very effective because it was thematically related to the film, it was unique (not the usual button, hat or T-shirt) and it was useful. Indeed, acquisition executives used the pad during the festival to take notes about the films they were viewing. And every time they picked up their pad, they were reminded about our film.

The filmmaker was on excellent terms with his cast and crew. Unlike some productions, everyone was still talking to one another. Ten of the filmmaker's collaborators attended the market at their own expense. The editor, composer, co-producers, and several of the stars of the film arrived in New York beforehand. They all pitched in and passed out leaflets, asked nearby store owners to display the film's poster and approached buyers inviting them to attend our screenings. The effort resembled a political campaign, and as a result of this work, 57 buyers attended our first screening and strong positive word-of-mouth was generated. The film was subsequently invited to exhibit at the Hamptons Film Festival where it won the top prize, which came with a $110,000 grant of services toward the filmmaker's next film.

Once you are able to interest distributors in your film, you must be careful not to compromise your bargaining position. It is important not to brag about how little money you spent to make your film before you conclude your distribution deal. You may feel justly proud of making a great-looking picture for a mere $200,000. But if the distributor knows that is all you have spent, you will find it difficult to get an advance beyond that. It would be wiser not to reveal your investment, recognizing that production costs are not readily discernible from viewing a film. Remember, the distributor has no right to examine your books. What you have spent is between you, your investors and the I.R.S.

From the filmmaker's point of view, you will get the best distribution deal if you have more than one distributor interested in acquiring your movie. That way you can play one off another to get the best terms. But what if one distributor makes a pre-emptive bid for the film, offering you a $500,000 advance, and you have only twenty four hours to accept their offer? If you pass, you may not be able to get a better deal later. It is possible you may fail to obtain any distribution deal at all. On the other hand, if you accept the offer, you may be foreclosing the possibility of a more lucrative deal that could be offered you later. Consequently, it is important to orchestrate the release of your film to potential distributors to maximize your leverage. Here are some guidelines:

ORCHESTRATING THE RELEASE

• *Keep The Film Under Wraps*: Don't show your film until it is finished. Executives may ask to see a rough cut. They will say "don't worry. We're professionals, we can extrapolate and envision what the film will look like with sound and titles." Don't believe them. Most people can't extrapolate. They will view your unfinished film and think it amateurish. First impressions last.

The only reason to show your film before completion is if you are desperate to raise funds to finish it. The terms you can obtain under these circumstances will usually be less than those given on completion. If you must show a work in progress, exhibit it on a Moviola or flatbed editing table. People have lower expectations viewing a film on an editing console than when it is projected in a theater.

• *Arrange A Screening*: Invite executives to a screening; don't send them a videocassette. If you send a tape to a busy executive, he will pop it in his VCR. Ten minutes later the phone rings and he pushes the pause button. Then he watches another ten minutes until he is interrupted by his secretary. After being distracted ten times, he passes on your film because it is "too choppy." Well, of course it's choppy with all those interruptions.

You want to get the executive in a dark room, away from diversions, to view your film with a live audience—hopefully one that will respond positively. So if the film is not currently available for viewing at a festival, rent a screening room, invite all the acquisition executives you can, and pack the rest of the theater with your friends and relatives, especially Uncle Herb with his infectious laugh.

• *Make The Buyers Compete Against Each Other*: Screen the film for all distributors simultaneously. Some executives will attempt to get an early look—that is their job. Your job is to keep them intrigued until it is complete. You can promise to let them see it "as soon as it is finished." They may be annoyed to arrive at the screening and see their competitors. But this will get their competitive juices flowing. They will know that they better make a decent offer quickly if they hope to get the film.

•   *Obtain An Experienced Advisor:* Retain an experienced producer's rep or entertainment attorney to negotiate your deal. Filmmakers know about film, distributors know about distribution. Don't kid yourself and believe you can play in their arena and win. There are many pitfalls to avoid. Get yourself an experienced guide to protect your interests. Any decent negotiator can improve a distributor's offer enough to outweigh the cost of his services.

•   *Investigate The Distributor:* Always check the track record and experience of potential distributors. As an entertainment attorney who represents many independent filmmakers, I often find myself in the position of trying to get unscrupulous distributors to live up to their contracts. I am amazed how many distributors refuse to abide by the clear terms of their own distribution agreements. The savvy filmmaker will carefully investigate potential distributors by calling filmmakers who have contracted with them. One can also check the Superior Court dockets where the distributor is incorporated to see if a company has been sued.

CHECKLIST FOR SELECTING A DISTRIBUTOR

1.   Amount of advance.

2.   Extent of rights conveyed. Domestic and/or foreign. Ancillary rights? Are any markets cross-collateralized?

3.   Is there a guaranteed marketing commitment?

4.   Does the producer have any input or veto power over artwork and theater selection in the top markets?

5.   Track record and financial health of distributor?

6.   Are monthly or quarterly accounting statements required?

7.   To what extent does the distributor plan to involve the filmmakers in promotion?

8.   Marketing strategy: demographics of intended market, grassroots promotion efforts, film festivals, etc.?

9.   Split of revenues and accounting of profits: is there a distribution fee? Overhead fees?

10. Distributor leverage with exhibitors. Can the distributor collect monies owed?

11. Any competing films handled by distributor? Conflicts of interest?

12. Does the producer have the right to regain distribution rights if the distributor pulls the plug early on distribution?

13. Personal chemistry between producer and distribution executives.

THE ACQUISITION/ DISTRIBUTION AGREEMENT

Mark Litwak

here are several ways to develop or produce a film. Beginning with an idea, or the movie rights to an existing literary property, a studio can hire a writer to create a script. The studio's development staff works with the writer to craft the story. Most of the scripts developed by studios, however, never get produced.

Other movies begin with a script developed outside the studio. Here a writer, working on his own or hired by an independent producer, writes a screenplay. After it is finished, it may be packaged (joined) with other elements (e.g., a star or director) and presented to the studio for financing and distribution. The big three talent agencies (CAA, ICM, and William Morris) are responsible for most packaging.

Other films are both developed and produced away from the studio that ultimately distributes them. These independently produced projects are often dependent on investors or pre-sale distribution deals (selling off various foreign distribution rights) to finance production. The producer then enters an acquisition agreement with a distributor for release of the picture. This is called a *negative pick-up deal*.

While the terms of negative pick-up deals vary, the studio/distributor typically pays for all distribution, advertising and marketing costs. The studio and producer share profits. Because the producer has taken the risk of financing production, he probably can obtain a better definition of net profits than if he made the film with studio financing. Profits may be split 50/50 between the studio and producer without a deduction for a studio distribution fee. Of course, the independent producer takes the risk that if the film turns out poorly, no distributor will want it. Then the producer can incur a substantial loss.

In a negative pick-up deal, the distributor may agree to give the producer an advance of his share of the profits. The producer can use this money to repay investors. Producers will want to obtain as large an advance as possible because they know they may never see anything on the back end of the deal (i.e., no profits).

The distributor wants to pay as small an advance as possible, and usually resists giving an amount that is more than the cost of production. · Its executives will propose "We'll be partners. We will put up all the money for advertising and promotion. If the picture is successful we will share in its success." Sound good?

Unfortunately, distributors have been known to engage in creative accounting, and profit participants rarely see any return on their share of "net profits" because of the way that term is defined. Consequently, the shrewd producer tries to get as large an advance as possible. He also tries to retain foreign rights and keep them from being cross-collateralized so that expenses from different territories are not pooled. For example, let's say your picture made one million dollars in England and lost one million dollars in France. If those territories were cross-collateralized, and you were entitled to a percentage of the net revenue after expenses, you would get nothing. On the other hand, if the territories were not cross-collateralized, you would get your percentage of the English revenues and the distributor would absorb the loss incurred in France.

Here are some problem areas to watch out for when reviewing a studio's accounting:

Excessive Bills: If the studio used a film lab that is a subsidiary, has the film processing been charged at the prevailing rate? If the studio has used its own vehicles in a shoot, is it fair for them to charge the production the highest daily rate that Hertz might charge?

Rebates: If a studio receives year-end rebates, have all the films been credited with their fair share?

Overhead Charges: Studio overhead charges may apply even if a film is not shot on a studio lot. This fee is meant to compensate a studio for the fixed costs of running the production and for the corporate functions performed by the studio. Distributors also may charge a 10% advertising overhead charge, which is meant to reimburse the studio for the fixed costs of operating the marketing division. But what if all the advertising work is contracted out? Is it proper to take an overhead fee? What does the contract say?

Interest: Studios charge the production interest on money used to make each film. They often mark up the rate. For example, they may borrow the money at prime and charge you prime plus two. Does the contract allow this? Also, advances from exhibitors are often not credited against interest charged. Thus the studio collects interest on advances while refusing to credit this interest against the interest charged the producer.

Misallocation of Expenses: It is in the studio's interest to tack on expenses to successful pictures to avoid having to pay profit participants. Unsuccessful pictures will never earn enough revenue to pay participants under any circumstances. Thus the cost of limos, lunches, executive travel and other expenses that were incurred on flops may find their way onto the books of hits.

Misallocation of Revenues: If the studio sells a package of its films to television, how have the revenues been allocated? If one film is a hit and the others are flops, is it fair to apportion the revenue equally among the pictures? The studios prefer to allocate revenue to flops that have no chance of earning a profit to avoid paying profit participants.

Home Video: Many studios have home video subsidiaries. These subsidiaries will typically pay the studio 20% of the wholesale price as a royalty for the right to distribute the movie in the home video market. The royalty payments are then added to the studio's gross receipts, and a distribution fee deducted. Is it fair for the studio to license the product to its own subsidiary for only 20%? Is it fair for both the subsidiary and the parent company to each make a profit from home video distribution?

Advertising and Merchandising Revenue: The studio may earn a fee from putting a Coca-Cola commercial on its videocassettes. Or a manufacturer may pay to have a product shown in a picture. Has the studio accounted for this revenue? A studio may license a manufacturer to produce spin-off toys and merchandise. Has the studio accounted for all this revenue?

Foreign Dubs: Has the film been dubbed into a foreign language? Are the charges appropriate? What is the local practice? Pictures released in Japan, for example, are subtitled, not dubbed.

Taxes: Some governments impose a remittance tax on money taken out of the country. The U.S. government allows a credit on these taxes on the distributor's U.S. tax return. If the tax doesn't really cost the studio anything, should it be deductible?

Calculation of interest: Studios may charge interest on items that are not out-of-pocket expenses. Did the studio charge simple interest or compound interest? What is the period for which interest is charged? Is the studio assessing interest based on a 360-day year? If interest is tied to the prime rate, was it properly calculated? What does the contract say?

Payments to Gross Participants: Are these payments considered part of the negative cost? Will an overhead fee be assessed on it? Suppose the gross profit participants earn five million dollars. The studio could deduct an overhead fee of $750,000 for the task of writing and mailing a few checks.

Over Budget Penalty: This penalty may be added to negative cost, even if the studio was responsible for the film going over budget. Perhaps the budget never was realistic in the first place.

ACCOUNTING TERMS

Each studio can define the terms used in its agreements as it likes. There are no industry-wide definitions for "Gross," "Adjusted Gross" or "Net" deals. What one studio calls an adjusted gross deal, another calls a net deal. Before you celebrate the "Gross" deal you obtained, check the fine print and see how the term is defined. Generally, industry terms are defined as follows:

- *Box Office Receipts:* What the theater owner takes in from ticket sales to customers at the box office. A portion of this revenue is remitted to the studio/distributor in the form of rental payments.

- *Film Rental:* What the theater owner pays the distributor for the right to show the movie. As a rough rule of thumb, this usually amounts to about half of the box office gross.

- *Gross Receipts:* Studio/distributor revenues derived from all media, including film rentals, television sales, merchandising and ancillary sales. The amount of revenues contributed by home video sales, for example, is typically twenty percent of wholesale sales.

- *Gross Participation:* A piece of gross receipts without any deductions for distribution fees or expenses or production costs. However, deductions for checking and collection costs, residuals and taxes are usually deductible. A "piece of the gross" is the most advantageous type of participation from the filmmaker or writer's point of view. In an audit, it is the most easily verified form of participation. Keep in mind that the "gross" is gross film rentals, not box office gross.

- *First Dollar Gross:* The most favorable form of gross participation for the participant. Only a few deductions, such as checking fees, taxes and trade association dues are deductible.

- *Gross After Break-Even:* The participant shares in the gross after the break-even point has been reached. The break-even point can be a set amount or determined by a formula.

- *Adjusted Gross Participation:* Gross participation minus certain costs, such as cost of advertising and duplication. Also called "Rolling Gross." If many deductions are allowed, the participant is essentially getting a "net profit" deal.

- *Net Profit:* What is left, if anything, after allowable deductions are taken. This usually amounts to zero. Typically expressed in terms of 100% of net profits, although payable out of the producer's share (e.g., out of his 50%).

- *Advances:* Up-front payment that counts against monies that may be payable at some time in the future. Non-recoupable advances are payments that are not refundable even if future monies are never due.

- *Theatrical Distribution Fees:* Generally between 30% and 40% of gross film rentals.

- *Double Distribution Fees:* Where a distributor uses a sub-distributor to sell to a territory. If both distributors are allowed to deduct their standard fees, the filmmaker is less likely to see any money.

- *Television Distribution Fee:* Typically 10-25% for U.S. Network broadcast sales, 30-40% for domestic syndication and 45-50% for foreign distribution. Many filmmakers consider these fees excessive since the studio doesn't incur a lot of expense to distribute to television. There are minimal duplication expenses (i.e., the studio sends one video copy to the buyer).

• *Distribution Expenses:* Includes taxes, guild payments, trade association dues, conversion/transmission costs, collection costs, checking costs, advertising and publicity costs, re-editing costs, prints, foreign version costs, transportation and shipping costs, copyright costs, copyright infringement costs, insurance, royalties, and claims and lawsuits.

• *Negative Cost:* The cost of producing a film. It may be defined to include overhead expenses, interest and other expenses which may inflate the amount way beyond what was actually spent to make the film.

DEFENSIVE TACTICS

Read your contract carefully including any addendum of standard terms and conditions. Don't assume that the "standard" terms are either standard or non-negotiable.

Reduce or place caps on expense items such as overhead and interest charges.

Define profits in terms of 100% of all profits. Remove any ambiguity as to whether you are sharing in the producer's share of net profits or a percentage of the whole.

Audit rights should provide the participant with a reasonable length of time to challenge statements. A participant will not want to incur the expense of an audit until he is reasonably certain the picture can be profitable. Since revenue from many markets dribbles in over a long time, the participant should not be forced to either audit early or waive his rights. Also, the agreement should provide for reimbursement of audit costs and attorney fees if the participant successfully recovers as a result of studio accounting errors.

Arbitration is always preferable to litigation especially when your opponent is better able to finance a protracted court struggle. Make sure the arbitration clause provides for binding arbitration and reimbursement of attorney fees and costs.

Eliminate or reduce studio distribution fees especially when the studio is using a subsidiary company as a sub-distributor. For example, studios may distribute through a wholly-owned home video distributor. The home video distributor pays a 20% royalty on sales to the parent company. This revenue may then go into studio gross revenues and may be reduced further by the parent studio's distribution fee.

Advertising expenses should be carefully defined and should only include salaries for staffers assigned exclusively to the project for the time they actually worked on it. An overall cap on advertising expenses is also important to prevent the distributor from "buying the gross." It can be profitable for a studio to spend money to promote a picture yet be disadvantageous to profit participants. That is because the studio recoups its advertising expenses, and perhaps some overhead on it, before profits are available.

Reduce interest costs by the amount of interest earned by the studio on advances from exhibitors. It is not fair for the studio to earn interest on advances while charging the producer interest on the full outstanding negative cost.

Sub-distribution fees should be included in the studio's distribution fee. Distribution fees for outright sales to smaller territories should not exceed 15%. The contract needs to be carefully worded so that these sales are charged at the lower outright sale distribution fee even if the buyer is technically required to account to the studio for income.

Taxes should be deducted from gross revenues before the studio takes its distribution fee. Some countries assess a remittance tax on funds remitted to other countries. These taxes may be a tax credit for the distributor. Some distribution agreements allow the studio to deduct these taxes as a distribution expense.

SELF DEFENSE CHECKLIST

1. *Get All Promises In Writing:* Don't ever accept oral assurances from a producer or studio executive. If they promise to spend $50,000 in advertising, get it in writing. If there is not enough time to draft a long-form contract, obtain a letter reiterating their promises.

2. *Register All Works With The Writer's Guild:* Before you pitch a story, register the work with the Writer's Guild. Non-members may register. Alternatively, register your work with the Copyright Office.

3. *Obtain An Arbitration Clause:* Make sure all contractual disputes are subject to binding arbitration with the prevailing party entitled to reimbursement of legal fees and costs.

4. *Water Down The Warranties:* Make the warranties to the best of your knowledge and belief, rather than absolute. With an absolute warranty, if you make a good faith mistake and defame another, you may be liable for damages.

5. *Retain Possession Of Your Negative:* Give the distributor a lab access letter rather than your original negative. If they breach your contract, you can cut off their access to the negative. Try to retain your original still photos and any artwork.

6. *Get Added To The E & O Policy:* Have yourself added as a named insured to the Errors and Omissions Insurance policy. If you are on the policy, the insurance company will pay for your defense and damages that may arise from liability if you inadvertently defame someone or infringe their copyright.

7. *Check References:* The best contract in the world can only protect you so much against a scoundrel. Thoroughly check out any party you contemplate doing business with. For distributors call other filmmakers who have worked with them. People who have lousy reputations have earned them.

8. *Termination Clause:* If the other party defaults you should have the right to terminate the contract and regain all rights to your film in addition to monetary damages. Writers should insist on a reversion clause so if a script is bought and not produced within five years, all rights revert to the writer.

9. *Investor Money:* Never make any "offers" to investors or accept any investor money without fully complying with all applicable state and federal security laws. Have an entertainment attorney with experience in securities prepare the paperwork for you.

10. *Save Copies:* Retain copies of all correspondence, contracts and every draft of your screenplay. When you make a story contribution or make an oral agreement, follow up with a letter reiterating the terms of your agreement.

MARK LITWAK is an entertainment and multimedia attorney with the Beverly Hills law firm of Berton & Donaldson. He has acted as a producer's rep for numerous independent features. He is the author of many articles and four books including *Reel Power, The Struggle for Influence and Success in the New Hollywood, Dealmaking in the Motion Picture and Television Industry,* and *Contracts in the Motion Picture and Television Industry.* Mr. Litwak can be reached by phone at (310) 859-9595; fax: (310) 859-0806; e-mail: Litwak@aol.com.

ACTION/ADVENTURE

ABC Distribution Company
Adler Media
Amazing Movies
Arrow Entertainment, Inc.
Artistic License Films
Capital Communications
Castle Hill Productions
Cinema Classics
Cinequanon Releasing Corporation
Columbia TriStar Home Video
Concorde/New Horizons
CS Associates
Distant Horizon Corporation
DMS Export Import
Filmopolis Pictures
Films Around the World/Filmworld
    Television, Inc.
Fox Lorber Associates, Inc.
Fries Distribution Company
Glenn Photo Supply/Glenn Video
    Vistas, Ltd.
Gramercy Pictures
Greycat Films
Hemdale Entertainment
International Creative Exchange
IRS Releasing
ITC Entertainment Group
Kino International Corporation
Leo Film Releasing
Live Entertainment
MCA/Universal Home Video
Miramax Films
New and Unique Videos
New Line Cinema
Northern Arts Entertainment, Inc.
Overseas Filmgroup

Kit Parker Films
Republic Pictures
RKO Pictures
Savoy Pictures
Seventh Art Releasing
Sony Pictures Classics, Inc.
Tara Releasing
Taurus Entertainment Company
Transcontinental Pictures Industries
Trident Releasing
Trimark Pictures
Triumph Films
Troma, Inc.
Vista Street Entertainment
Warner Home Video

ANIMATION

ABC Distribution Company
Alternative Videos
ATA Trading Corporation
Canyon Cinema
The Cinema Guild
Coe Film Associates
Devillier Donegan Enterprises
Direct Cinema, Ltd.
Expanded Entertainment
Facets Multimedia
Film-Makers' Cooperative
Films Around the World/Filmworld
    Television, Inc.
International Creative Exchange
Italtoons Corporation
Arthur Mokin Productions, Inc.
Kit Parker Films
Phoenix Films and Video
Picture Start, Inc.

Public Media Home Video/Public
 Media Education
Chip Taylor Communications
Warner Home Video
Women Make Movies
Zeitgeist Films, Ltd.

ARCHIVAL

Canyon Cinema
The Cinema Guild
Darino Films
Electronic Arts Intermix
Film-Makers' Cooperative
Films Around the World/Filmworld
 Television, Inc.
Glenn Photo Supply/Glenn Video
 Vistas, Ltd.
Ivy Film and Video
Kino International Corporation
Museum of Modern Art
Kit Parker Films
Third World Newsreel
Video Data Bank

ARTS

ABC Distribution Company
ATA Trading Corporation
Barr Media Group
Bullfrog Films
Arthur Cantor Films, Inc.
Canyon Cinema
Capital Communications
Carousel Film and Video
Churchill Media
The Cinema Guild
Coe Film Associates

Corinth Video
Direct Cinema, Ltd.
Drift Releasing
Electronic Arts Intermix
Expanded Entertainment
Facets Multimedia
Filmmakers Library
Film-Makers' Cooperative
Films Around the World/Filmworld
 Television, Inc.
Films for the Humanities and
 Sciences, Inc.®
Flower Films and Video
Fox Lorber Associates, Inc.
Glenn Photo Supply/Glenn Video
 Vistas, Ltd.
International Film Circuit
Kino International Corporation
The Kitchen Video Distribution
 Collection
KJM3 Entertainment Group, Inc.
Milestone Film and Video
Museum of Modern Art
Myriad Pictures
Mystic Fire Video
NAATA/Cross Current Media
National Black Programming
 Consortium
New Day Films
New Dimension Media Inc.
Pacific Islanders in Communications
Parabola Arts Foundation
Kit Parker Films
Pathe News, Inc./Pathe Pictures, Inc.
PBS Video
Phoenix Films and Video
Public Media Home Video/Public
 Media Education

Pyramid Film and Video
Rhapsody Films, Inc.
Strand Releasing
Tapestry International, Ltd.
Chip Taylor Communications
Third World Newsreel
Video Data Bank
Videodisc Publishing, Inc./VPI/AC
    Video, Inc.
Vision Makers Video
Women Make Movies
Zeitgeist Films, Ltd.

CHILDREN'S MEDIA

ABC Distribution Company
Adler Media
Altschul Group Corporation
ATA Trading Corporation
Bullfrog Films
Bureau for At-Risk Youth
Carousel Film and Video
Churchill Media
The Cinema Guild
Coe Film Associates
CS Associates
Devillier Donegan Enterprises
Educational Productions, Inc.
Educational Video Center
Expanded Entertainment
Facets Multimedia
Filmmakers Library
Films for the Humanities and
    Sciences, Inc.®
GPN/University of Nebraska
International Creative Exchange
Italtoons Corporation

Kit Parker Films
MCA/Universal Home Video
Arthur Mokin Productions, Inc.
New Dimension Media Inc.
PBS Video
Phoenix Films and Video
Public Media Home Video/Public
    Media Education
Select Media, Inc.
Tapestry International, Ltd.
Chip Taylor Communications
United Nations Audio Visual
    Promotion and Distribution
The Video Project
Warner Home Video

COMEDY, FANTASY, MYSTERY, THRILLER

ABC Distribution Company
Alternative Videos
Arrow Entertainment, Inc.
Castle Hill Productions
Cinema Classics
Cinequanon Releasing Corporation
Columbia TriStar Home Video
Concorde/New Horizons
Devillier Donegan Enterprises
Distant Horizon Corporation
DMS Export Import
Facets Multimedia
Fox Lorber Associates, Inc.
Fries Distribution Company
Glenn Photo Supply/Glenn Video
    Vistas, Ltd.
Samuel Goldwyn Company
Gramercy Pictures
Greycat Films

Hemdale Entertainment
Interama Video Classics
IRS Releasing
ITC Entertainment Group
Ivy Film and Video
Kino International Corporation
Live Entertainment
MCA/Universal Home Video
Milestone Film and Video
National Black Programming
  Consortium
New Line Cinema
Northern Arts Entertainment, Inc.
October Films
Original Cinema
Pacific Islanders in Communications
Panorama Entertainment
  Corporation
Kit Parker Films
Picture Start, Inc.
Republic Pictures
RKO Pictures
Sony Pictures Classics, Inc.
Strand Releasing
Tapeworm Video Distributors
Tara Releasing
Transcontinental Pictures Industries
Trident Releasing
Troma, Inc.
Warner Home Video

DOCUMENTARY— ALL LENGTHS

ABC Distribution Company
Adler Media
James Agee Film Project

AIMS Media
Alternative Videos
Ambrose Video Publishing, Inc.
Appalshop Film and Video
ATA Trading Corporation
Barr Media Group
Baxley Media Group
Bullfrog Films
Bureau for At-Risk Youth
California Newsreel
Cambridge Documentary Films
Arthur Cantor Films, Inc.
Canyon Cinema
Carousel Film and Video
Churchill Media
The Cinema Guild
Coe Film Associates
Concept Media
Cornell University Audio-Visual
  Resource Center
CS Associates
Darino Films
Devillier Donegan Enterprises
Direct Cinema, Ltd.
Educational Video Center
The Educational Video Group
Fanlight Productions
Film Ideas, Inc.
Filmmakers Library
Film-Makers' Cooperative
Films for Educators, Inc./Films for
  Television
Films for the Humanities and
  Sciences, Inc.®
First Run Features and First
  Run/Icarus
Flower Films and Video
Fox Lorber Associates, Inc.

Glenn Photo Supply/Glenn Video Vistas, Ltd.

GPN/University of Nebraska

Greycat Films

Intermedia

International Film Circuit

ITC Entertainment Group

Ivy Film

Kino International Corporation

The Kitchen Video Distribution Collection

Manbeck Pictures Corporation

Maryknoll World Productions

Media Guild

Media Methods

Merrimack Films

Milestone Film and Video, Inc.

Arthur Mokin Productions, Inc.

Museum of Modern Art

Mypheduh Films, Inc.

Myriad Pictures

Mystic Fire Video

NAATA/Cross Current Media

National Black Programming Consortium

National Geographic Television

New and Unique Videos

New Day Films

New Dimension Media Inc.

Pacific Islanders in Communications

Panorama Entertainment Corporation

Paper Tiger Television

Parabola Arts Foundation

Pathe News, Inc./Pathe Pictures, Inc.

PBS Video

Phoenix Films and Video

Public Media Home Video/Public Media Education

Pyramid Film and Video

Rhapsody Films, Inc.

Select Media, Inc.

Tapestry International, Ltd.

Chip Taylor Communications

Third World Newsreel

United Nations Audio Visual Promotion and Distribution

University of California Extension Center for Media and Independent Learning

Video Data Bank

Videodisc Publishing, Inc./VPI/AC Video, Inc.

The Video Project

Vision Makers Video

Women Make Movies

Zeitgeist Films, Ltd.

DOCUMENTARY— FEATURES ONLY

Angelika Films

Arrow Entertainment, Inc.

Artistic License Films

Capital Communications

Cinepix Film Properties, Inc.

Cinevista, Inc.

DMS Export Import

Drift Releasing

Filmopolis Pictures

Films Around the World/Filmworld Television, Inc.

Fries Distribution Company

International Creative Exchange

KJM3 Entertainment Group, Inc.

Leo Film Releasing
Milestone Film and Video
Miramax Films
New Yorker Films
Northern Arts Entertainment, Inc.
Outsider Enterprises
Kit Parker Films
Passport Cinemas, Ltd.
Roxie Releasing
Seventh Art Releasing
Sony Pictures Classics, Inc.

Phoenix Films and Video
Picture Start, Inc.
Pyramid Film and Video
Rhapsody Films, Inc.
Strand Releasing
Tapestry International, Ltd.
Tapeworm Video Distributors
Third World Newsreel
Video Data Bank
Vision Makers Video
Women Make Movies
Zeitgeist Films, Ltd.

EXPERIMENTAL/ AVANT-GARDE

Artistic License Films
Canyon Cinema
The Cinema Guild
Direct Cinema, Ltd.
Drift Releasing
Electronic Arts Intermix
Film-Makers' Cooperative
Glenn Photo Supply/Glenn Video
  Vistas, Ltd.
The Kitchen Video Distribution
  Collection
Milestone Film and Video, Inc.
Museum of Modern Art
Mystic Fire Video
NAATA/Cross Current Media
National Black Programming
  Consortium
New Day Films
Niteclub Video/Oddball Film and
  Video
Outsider Enterprises
Pacific Islanders in Communications
Paper Tiger Television

FAMILY

ABC Distribution Company
Adler Media
ATA Trading Corporation
Barr Media Group
Baxley Media Group
Bullfrog Films
Carousel Film and Video
Castle Hill Productions
Churchill Media
Clearvue
Coe Film Associates
CS Associates
Devillier Donegan Enterprises
Educational Productions, Inc.
The Educational Video Group
Expanded Entertainment
Filmmakers Library
Films Around the World/Filmworld
  Television, Inc.
Films for the Humanities and
  Sciences, Inc.®
Fox Lorber Associates, Inc.

GPN/University of Nebraska
Intermedia
International Creative Exchange
Italtoons Corporation
ITC Entertainment Group
Ivy Film and Video
KJM3 Entertainment Group, Inc.
Live Entertainment
MCA/Universal Home Video
Multimedia Entertainment, Inc.
Mypheduh Films, Inc.
NAATA/Cross Current Media
National Black Programming
   Consortium
Original Cinema
Pacific Islanders in Communications
Kit Parker Films
Phoenix Films and Video
Picture Start, Inc.
Public Media Home Video/Public
   Media Education
Pyramid Film and Video
Republic Pictures
Select Media, Inc.
Tapestry International, Ltd.
Chip Taylor Communications
Videodisc Publishing, Inc./VPI/AC
   Video, Inc.
Vision Makers Video
Warner Home Video

FEATURE, INDEPENDENT

A-Pix/Unapix Entertainment, Inc.
Alternative Videos
Amazing Movies
Arrow Entertainment, Inc.
Artistic License Films

ATA Trading Corporation
California Newsreel
Castle Hill Productions
The Cinema Guild
Cinepix Film Properties, Inc.
Cinequanon Releasing Corporation
Cinevista, Inc.
Direct Cinema, Ltd.
Distant Horizon Corporation
Drift Releasing
Facets Multimedia
FilmHaus
Filmopolis Pictures
Films Around the World/Filmworld
   Television, Inc.
First Run Features and First
   Run/Icarus
Fox Lorber Associates, Inc.
Samuel Goldwyn Company
Gramercy Pictures
Greycat Films
Home Film Festival
International Film Circuit
IRS Releasing
ISA Releasing, Ltd.
Italtoons Corporation
Ivy Film
Kino International Corporation
KJM3 Entertainment Group, Inc.
Milestone Film and Video, Inc.
Miramax Films
Mypheduh Films, Inc.
NAATA/Cross Current Media
National Black Programming
   Consortium
New Line Cinema
New Yorker Films
Northern Arts Entertainment, Inc.

October Films
Original Cinema
Orion Pictures - Classic Division
Outsider Enterprises
Overseas Filmgroup
Pacific Islanders in Communications
Panorama Entertainment
  Corporation
Kit Parker Films
Passport Cinemas, Ltd.
Public Media Home Video/Public
  Media Education
Republic Pictures
Roxie Releasing
Savoy Pictures
Seventh Art Releasing
Sony Pictures Classics, Inc.
Strand Releasing
Tapestry International, Ltd.
Tara Releasing
Third World Newsreel
Trident Releasing
Trimark Pictures
Triumph Films
Upstate Films
Vision Makers Video
Women Make Movies
Zeitgeist Films, Ltd.

FEATURE, THEATRICAL

A-Pix/Unapix Entertainment, Inc.
Amazing Movies
Angelika Films
Arrow Entertainment, Inc.
Artistic License Films
Castle Hill Productions

Cinepix Film Properties, Inc.
Cinequanon Releasing Corporation
Cinevista, Inc.
Concorde/New Horizons
Curb Entertainment International
  Corp.
Direct Cinema, Ltd.
Distant Horizon Corporation
Dream Entertainment
Drift Releasing
Entertainment Studios, Inc.
FilmHaus
Filmopolis Pictures
Films Around the World/Filmworld
  Television, Inc.
First Look Pictures Releasing
First Run Features and First
  Run/Icarus
Fox Searchlight Pictures
Fries Distribution Company
Samuel Goldwyn Company
Gramercy Pictures
Greycat Films
Hemdale Entertainment
International Film Circuit
IRS Releasing
ISA Releasing, Ltd.
ITC Entertainment Group
Italtoons Corporation
Ivy Film and Video
Kino International Corporation
KJM3 Entertainment Group, Inc.
Leo Film Releasing
Live Entertainment
Milestone Film and Video
Miramax Films
MLR Films International
Mypheduh Films, Inc.

New Line Cinema

New Yorker Films

Northern Arts Entertainment, Inc.

October Films

Original Cinema

Orion Pictures - Classic Division

Outsider Enterprises

Overseas Filmgroup

Panorama Entertainment
Corporation

Kit Parker Films

Rainbow Releasing

Raven Pictures International

Republic Pictures

Rigel Independent Distribution and
Entertainment

RKO Pictures

Roxie Releasing

Savoy Pictures

Seventh Art Releasing

Shadow Distribution

Silverstein International Corporation

Sony Pictures Classics, Inc.

Strand Releasing

Swank Motion Pictures

Tara Releasing

Taurus Entertainment Company

The Cinema Guild

Transcontinental Pictures Industries

Trident Releasing

Trimark Pictures

Triumph Films

Troma, Inc.

Women Make Movies

Zeitgeist Films, Ltd.

FOREIGN DISTRIBUTION/ INTERNATIONAL SALES AGENT

Amazing Movies

ATA Trading Corporation

Bullfrog Films

Churchill Media

Cinevista, Inc.

Coe Film Associates

Columbia TriStar Home Video

CS Associates

Curb Entertainment International
Corp.

Darino Films

Devillier Donegan Enterprises

Distant Horizon Corporation

Electronic Arts Intermix

First Run Features and First
Run/Icarus

Fox Lorber Associates, Inc.

International Creative Exchange

Italtoons Corporation

Ivy Film

KJM3 Entertainment Group, Inc.

Arthur Mokin Productions, Inc.

Myriad Pictures

Overseas Filmgroup

Panorama Entertainment
Corporation

Pyramid Film and Video

Tapestry International, Ltd.

United Nations Audio Visual
Promotion and Distribution

Video Data Bank

HEALTH, MEDICAL, ENVIRONMENTAL, SCIENTIFIC

James Agee Film Project
AIMS Media
Altschul Group Corporation
Ambrose Video Publishing, Inc.
Appalshop Film and Video
ATA Trading Corporation
Barr Media Group
Baxley Media Group
Bullfrog Films
Bureau for At-Risk Youth
Cambridge Documentary Films
Capital Communications
Carousel Film and Video
Chip Taylor Communications
Churchill Media
The Cinema Guild
Concept Media
Cornell University Audio-Visual Resource Center
CS Associates
Darino Films
Devillier Donegan Enterprises
Educational Productions, Inc.
Educational Video Center
Environmental Media Corporation
ETR Associates
Fanlight Productions
Film Ideas, Inc.
Film-Makers' Cooperative
Filmmakers Library
Films Around the World/Filmworld Television, Inc.
Films for Ediucators, Inc./Films for Television

Films for the Humanities and Sciences, Inc.®
GPN/University of Nebraska
Human Relations Media
Independent Video Services
Intermedia
International Video Network
Medfilms, Inc.
Media Guild
Media Methods
Arthur Mokin Productions, Inc.
National Geographic Television
New and Unique Videos
New Day Films
New Dimension Media Inc.
Paper Tiger Television
PBS Video
Phoenix Films and Video
Public Media Home Video/Public Media Education
Pyramid Film and Video
Select Media, Inc.
Tapestry International, Ltd.
Third World Newsreel
United Nations Audio Visual Promotion and Distribution
University of California Extension Center for Media and Independent Learning
The Video Project
Women Make Movies

HOME VIDEO

A-Pix/Unapix Entertainment, Inc.
Adler Media
AIMS Media
Amazing Movies
Ambrose Video Publishing, Inc.

Arrow Entertainment, Inc.
ATA Trading Corporation
California Newsreel
Arthur Cantor Films, Inc.
Chip Taylor Communications
Cinepix Film Properties, Inc.
Cinevista, Inc.
Columbia TriStar Home Video
Darino Films
Distant Horizon Corporation
Expanded Entertainment
Facets Multimedia
Filmopolis Pictures
First Run Features and
    First Run/Icarus
Fox Lorber Associates, Inc.
International Creative Exchange
International Film Circuit
International Video Network
ITC Entertainment Group
Ivy Film
Kino International Corporation
Kit Parker Films
The Kitchen Video Distribution
    Collection
KJM3 Entertainment Group, Inc.
Leo Film Releasing
Live Entertainment
MCA/Universal Home Video
Media Methods
Miramax Films
MLR Films International
Mypheduh Films, Inc.
Mystic Fire Video
National Black Programming
    Consortium
New and Unique Videos
New Line Cinema

New Yorker Films
Pacific Islanders in Communications
Pathe News, Inc./Pathe Pictures, Inc.
PBS Video
Phoenix Films and Video
Public Media Home Video/Public
    Media Education
Raven Pictures International
Sony Pictures Classics, Inc.
The Cinema Guild
Transcontinental Pictures Industries
Trident Releasing
University of California Extension
    Center for Media and
    Independent Learning
Video Data Bank
Vision Makers Video
Vision Video/Gateway Films, Inc.
Vista Street Entertainment
Warner Home Video
Zeitgeist Films, Ltd.

MULTI/CROSS-CULTURAL

California Newsreel
Canyon Cinema
KJM3 Entertainment Group, Inc.
Maryknoll World Productions
Milestone Film and Video, Inc.
Mypheduh Films
NAATA/Cross Current Media
National Black Programming
    Consortium
New Yorker Films
Pacific Islanders in Communications
PBS Video
Third World Newsreel
Vision Makers Video
Women Make Movies

MUSIC

Alternative Videos
ATA Trading Corporation
Arthur Cantor Films, Inc.
Capital Communications
Carousel Film and Video
Cinema Classics
Clearvue
CS Associates
Devillier Donegan Enterprises
Direct Cinema, Ltd.
Flower Films and Video
Fries Distribution Company
ITC Entertainment Group
Myriad Pictures
NAATA/Cross Current Media
National Black Programming
    Consortium
New Dimension Media Inc.
Pathe News, Inc./Pathe Pictures, Inc.
PBS Video
Phoenix Films and Video
Picture Start, Inc.
Premier Studios
Public Media Home Video/Public
    Media Education
Pyramid Film and Video
Rhapsody Films, Inc.
University of California Extension
    Center for Media and
    Independent Learning

NONTHEATRICAL, EDUCATIONAL

Adler Media
James Agee Film Project

AIMS Media
Altschul Group Corporation
Ambrose Video Publishing, Inc.
Appalshop Film and Video
ATA Trading Corporation
Barr Media Group
Baxley Media Group
Bullfrog Films
California Newsreel
Cambridge Documentary Films
Arthur Cantor Films, Inc.
Canyon Cinema
Carousel Film and Video
Chip Taylor Communications
Churchill Media
The Cinema Guild
Clearvue
Coe Film Associates
Concept Media
Cornell University Audio-Visual
    Resource Center
CRM Films
Darino Films
Devillier Donegan Enterprises
Direct Cinema, Ltd.
Educational Productions, Inc.
Educational Video Center
The Educational Video Group
Electronic Arts Intermix
Environmental Media Corporation
ETR Associates
Expanded Entertainment
Fanlight Productions
Film Ideas, Inc.
Filmmakers Library
Film-Makers' Cooperative

Films Around the World/Filmworld Television, Inc.

Films for Educators, Inc./Films for Television

Films for the Humanities and Sciences, Inc.®

First Run Features and First Run/Icarus

Flower Films and Video

Fox Lorber Associates, Inc.

Glenn Photo Supply/Glenn Video Vistas, Ltd.

GPN/University of Nebraska

Guidance Associates

Human Relations Media

Independent Video Services

Intermedia

International Film Circuit

International Film Foundation

International Video Network

Italtoons Corporation

Ivy Film and Video

Kino International Corporation

Kit Parker Films

The Kitchen Video Distribution Collection

KJM3 Entertainment Group, Inc.

Landmark Media

Lucerne Media

Manbeck Pictures Corporation

Maryknoll World Productions

Medfilms, Inc.

Media Guild

Media Methods

Merrimack Films

Museum of Modern Art

Mypheduh Films, Inc.

Myriad Pictures

Mystic Fire Video

NAATA/Cross Current Media

National Black Programming Consortium

New and Unique Videos

New Day Films

New Dimension Media Inc.

New Yorker Films

Northern Arts Entertainment, Inc.

Outsider Enterprises

Pacific Islanders in Communications

Panorama Entertainment Corporation

Pathe News, Inc./Pathe Pictures, Inc.

PBS Video

Phoenix Films and Video

Picture Start, Inc.

Premier Studios

Public Media Home Video/Public Media Education

Pyramid Film and Video

Rhapsody Films, Inc.

Select Media, Inc.

Strand Releasing

Sunburst Communications, Inc.

Swank Motion Pictures

Tapestry International, Ltd.

Third World Newsreel

United Nations Audio Visual Promotion and Distribution

University of California Extension Center for Media and Independent Learning

Video Data Bank

The Video Project

Vision Makers Video

Vision Video/Gateway Films, Inc.

Vocational Marketing Services (VMS)

Women Make Movies
Zeitgeist Films, Ltd.
Zenger Media

SHORT

Ambrose Video Publishing, Inc.
ATA Trading Corporation
Barr Media Group
Bullfrog Films
Canyon Cinema
Capital Communications
Carousel Film and Video
Chip Taylor Communications
Churchill Media
The Cinema Guild
CS Associates
Darino Films
Devillier Donegan Enterprises
Direct Cinema, Ltd.
The Educational Video Group
Film Ideas, Inc.
Filmmakers Library
Film-Makers' Cooperative
Films for Educators, Inc./Films for
    Television
Films for the Humanities and
    Sciences, Inc.®
Flower Films and Video
GPN/University of Nebraska
International Film Circuit
Ivy Film
The Kitchen Video Distribution
    Collection
Manbeck Pictures Corporation
Arthur Mokin Productions, Inc.
Museum of Modern Art
Myriad Pictures

NAATA/Cross Current Media
National Black Programming
    Consortium
New Day Films
Pacific Islanders in Communications
Passport Cinemas, Ltd.
Pathe News, Inc./Pathe Pictures, Inc.
PBS Video
Phoenix Films and Video
Public Media Home Video/Public
    Media Education
Pyramid Film and Video
Tapestry International, Ltd.
United Nations Audio Visual
    Promotion and Distribution
University of California Extension
    Center for Media and
    Independent Learning
Video Data Bank
Videodisc Publishing, Inc./VPI/AC
    Video, Inc.
The Video Project
Vision Makers Video
Women Make Movies
Zeitgeist Films, Ltd.

TELEVISION, DOMESTIC

A-Pix/Unapix Entertainment, Inc.
ABC Distribution Company
AIMS Media
Amazing Movies
Arrow Entertainment, Inc.
ATA Trading Corporation
Barr Media Group
Baxley Media Group
Bullfrog Films
California Newsreel

Capital Communications

Churchill Media

The Cinema Guild

Cinepix Film Properties, Inc.

Cinevista, Inc.

Coe Film Associates

CS Associates

Devillier Donegan Enterprises

Distant Horizon Corporation

DMS Export Import

Electronic Arts Intermix

Expanded Entertainment

Fanlight Productions

Film Ideas, Inc.

Filmopolis Pictures

Films Around the World/Filmworld Television, Inc.

First Run Features and First Run/Icarus

Fox Lorber Associates, Inc.

Samuel Goldwyn Company

Independent Video Services

International Creative Exchange

International Film Circuit

Italtoons Corporation

ITC Entertainment Group

Ivy Film

The Kitchen Video Distribution Collection

KJM3 Entertainment Group, Inc.

Live Entertainment

Milestone Film and Video, Inc.

Miramax Films

MLR Films International

Arthur Mokin Productions, Inc.

Multimedia Entertainment, Inc.

Mypheduh Films, Inc.

Myriad Pictures

NAATA/Cross Current Media

National Black Programming Consortium

National Geographic Television

New Line Cinema

New Yorker Films

Northern Arts Entertainment, Inc.

Outsider Enterprises

Pacific Islanders in Communications

Paper Tiger Television

Kit Parker Films

Passport Cinemas, Ltd.

Pathe News, Inc./Pathe Pictures, Inc.

PBS Video

Phoenix Films and Video

Public Media Home Video/Public Media Education

Pyramid Film and Video

Raven Pictures International

Republic Pictures

Rigel Independent Distribution and Entertainment

Savoy Pictures

Sony Pictures Classics, Inc.

Strand Releasing

Tapestry International, Ltd.

Taurus Entertainment Company

Chip Taylor Communications

Third World Newsreel

Trident Releasing

United Nations Audio Visual Promotion and Distribution

Video Data Bank

The Video Project

Vision Makers Video

Women Make Movies

Zeitgeist Films, Ltd.

TELEVISION, FOREIGN

ABC Distribution Company
Arrow Entertainment, Inc.
ATA Trading Corporation
Barr Media Group
Coe Film Associates
CS Associates
Darino Films
Devillier Donegan Enterprises
Distant Horizon Corporation
DMS Export Import
Electronic Arts Intermix
Expanded Entertainment
Films Around the World/Filmworld
    Television, Inc.
First Run Features and First
    Run/Icarus
Fox Lorber Associates, Inc.
Independent Video Services
International Creative Exchange
Italtoons Corporation
ITC Entertainment Group
Ivy Film
KJM3 Entertainment Group, Inc.
Live Entertainment
Miramax Films
Myriad Pictures
National Geographic Television
New Line Cinema
Outsider Enterprises
Raven Pictures International
Republic Pictures
Rigel Independent Distribution and
    Entertainment
Sony Pictures Classics, Inc.
Tapestry International, Ltd.

Trident Releasing
United Nations Audio Visual
    Promotion and Distribution

VIDEO

ABC Distribution Company
Alternative Videos
Appalshop Film and Video
ATA Trading Corporation
Bureau for At-Risk Youth
California Newsreel
Arthur Cantor Films, Inc.
Canyon Cinema
Cinema Classics
The Cinema Guild
Cinepix Film Properties, Inc.
Coe Film Associates
Concept Media
Corinth Video
CS Associates
Direct Cinema, Ltd.
Electronic Arts Intermix
Fanlight Productions
Film-Makers' Cooperative
Films Around the World/Filmworld
    Television, Inc.
Films for the Humanities and
    Sciences, Inc.®
Fox Lorber Associates, Inc.
GPN/University of Nebraska
Home Film Festival
Independent Video Services
Interama Video Classics
International Film Circuit
Ivy Film and Video
Kino International Corporation

Kit Parker Films
The Kitchen Video Distribution
   Collection
Live Entertainment
Media Methods
Milestone Film and Video, Inc.
Myriad Pictures
Mystic Fire Video
NAATA/Cross Current Media
National Black Programming
   Consortium
New and Unique Videos
Pacific Islanders in Communications
Paper Tiger Television
Passport Cinemas, Ltd.
PBS Video
Phoenix Films and Video
Picture Start, Inc.
Rhapsody Films, Inc.
Tapestry International, Ltd.
Tapeworm Video Distributors
Taurus Entertainment Company
Third World Newsreel
University of California Extension
   Center for Media and
   Independent Learning
Video Data Bank
Vision Makers Video
Vocational Marketing Services (VMS)
Women Make Movies
Zenger Media

WOMEN

Artistic License Films
Baxley Media Group
Bullfrog Films
Cambridge Documentary Films
Canyon Cinema
Carousel Film and Video
Churchill Media
The Cinema Guild
Direct Cinema, Ltd.
Film-Makers' Cooperative
Filmmakers Library
First Run Features and First
   Run/Icarus
Intermedia
International Film Circuit
The Kitchen Video Distribution
   Collection
NAATA/Cross Current Media
National Black Programming
   Consortium
New Day Films
New Dimension Media Inc.
Pacific Islanders in Communications
Paper Tiger Television
PBS Video
Phoenix Films and Video
Pyramid Film and Video
Chip Taylor Communications
Third World Newsreel
United Nations Audio Visual
   Promotion and Distribution
University of California Extension
   Center for Media and
   Independent Learning
Video Data Bank
Vision Makers Video
Women Make Movies

A-Pix/Unapix Entertainment, Inc.
500 Fifth Avenue, 46th Floor
New York NY 10110
(212) 764-7171
Fax: (212) 575-6578

ABC Distribution Company
825 Seventh Avenue, 5th floor
New York NY 10019
(212) 456-1725
Fax: (212) 456-1708

Adler Media
6849 Old Dominion Drive,
    Suite 360
McLean VA 22101
(703) 556-8880
Fax: (703) 556-9288

James Agee Film Project
316 East Main Street
Johnson City TN 37601
(615) 926-8637
Fax: (804) 971-2921

AIMS Media
9710 DeSoto Avenue
Chatsworth CA 91311
(818) 773-4300/(800) 367-2467
Fax: (818) 376-6405

Alternative Videos
P.O. Box 270797
Dallas TX 75227
(214) 823-6030

Altschul Group Corporation
1560 Sherman Avenue, Suite 100
Evanston IL 60201
(708) 328-6700
Fax: (708) 328-6706
e-mail: agcmedia@starnet.nc.com

Amazing Movies
7471 Melrose Avenue, Suite 7
Los Angeles CA 90046
(213) 852-1396
Fax: (213) 658-7265

Ambrose Video Publishing, Inc.
1290 Avenue of the Americas
New York NY 10104
(212) 265-7272
Fax: (212) 265-8088

Angelika Films
110 Greene Street, Suite 1102
New York NY 10012
(212) 274-1990
Fax: (212) 966-4957

Appalshop Film and Video
306 Madison Street
Whitesburg KY 41858
(606) 633-0108
Fax: (606) 633-1009
e-mail: appalshop@aol.com

Arrow Entertainment, Inc.
One Rockefeller Plaza, 16th Floor
New York NY 10020
(212) 332-8140
Fax: (212) 332-8161

Artistic License Films
470 Park Avenue South, 9th Floor
New York NY 10016
(212) 251-8718
Fax: (212) 251-8606
e-mail: artlic@aol.com

ATA Trading Corporation
50 West 34th Street, Suite 5C6
New York NY 10001
(212) 594-6460
Fax: (212) 594-6461

Barr Media Group
P.O. Box 7878
12801 Schabarum Avenue
Irwindale CA 91706-7878
(818) 338-7878/(800) 234-7878
Fax: (818) 814-2672

Baxley Media Group
110 West Main Street
Urbana IL 61801-2700
(217) 384-4838
Fax: (217) 384-8280

Bullfrog Films
Box 149
Oley PA 19547
(610) 779-8226/(800) 543-FROG
Fax: (610) 370-1978
e-mail: bullfrog@igc.apc.org

Bureau for At-Risk Youth
645 New York Avenue
Huntington NY 11743
(516) 673-4584
Fax: (516) 673-4544

California Newsreel
149 Ninth Street, Suite 420
San Francisco CA 94103
(415) 621-6196
Fax: (415) 621-6522
e-mail: newsreel@ix.netcom.com

Cambridge Documentary Films
P.O. Box 385
Cambridge MA 02139
(617) 354-3677
Fax: (617) 899-9602

Arthur Cantor Films, Inc.
1501 Broadway, Suite 403
New York NY 10036
(212) 391-2650
Fax: (212) 391-2677

Canyon Cinema
2325 Third Street, Suite 338
San Francisco, CA 94107
(415) 626-2255

Capital Communications
P.O. Box 3459
Venice FL 34293
(800) 822-5678

Carousel Film and Video
260 Fifth Avenue, Suite 405
New York NY 10001
(212) 683-1660
Fax: (212) 683-1662

Castle Hill Productions
1414 Avenue of the Americas
New York, NY 10019
(212) 888-0080
Fax: (212) 644-0956

Churchill Media
12210 Nebraska Avenue
Los Angeles CA 90025
(310) 207-6600/(800) 334-7830
Fax: (310) 207-1330

Cinema Classics
P.O. Box 174
Village Station
New York NY 10014
(212) 675-6692
Fax: (212) 675-6594

The Cinema Guild
1697 Broadway, Suite 506
New York NY 10019
(212) 246-5522
Fax: (212) 246-5525

Cinepix Film Properties, Inc.
900 Broadway, Suite 800
New York NY 10003
(212) 995-9662
Fax: (212) 475-2284

Cinequanon Releasing Corporation
8489 West Third Street
Los Angeles, CA 90048
(213) 658-6043
Fax: (213) 658-6087

Cinevista, Inc.
560 West 43rd Street, Suite 8J
New York NY 10036
(212) 947-4373
Fax: (212) 947-0644

Clearvue
6465 North Avondale
Chicago IL 60631
(312) 775-9433
Fax: (312) 775-9855

Coe Film Associates
65 East 96th Street
New York NY 10128
(212) 831-5355
Fax: (212) 996-6728

Columbia TriStar Home Video
10202 West Washington Blvd.
Culver City CA 90232
(310) 280-8000
Fax: (310) 280-1724

Concorde/New Horizons
11600 San Vicente Boulevard
Los Angeles, CA 90025
(310) 826-0978

Concept Media
2493 DuBridge Avenue
Irvine CA 92714-5022
(714) 660-0727
Fax: (714) 660-0206

Corinth Video
34 Gansevoort Street
New York, NY 10014-1597
(800) 221-4720
Fax: (212) 929-0010

Cornell University Audio-Visual
    Resource Center
7-8 Business and Technology Park
Ithaca NY 14850
(607) 255-2090
Fax: (607) 255-9946
e-mail: dist_cent@cce.cornell.edu.

CRM Films
2215 Faraday Avenue
Carlsbad CA 92008
(619) 431-9800
Fax: (619) 931-5792

CS Associates
52 Simon Willard Road
Concord, MA 01742
(508) 287-6100
Fax: (508) 287-6161
e-mail: csa@tiac.net
102 E. Blithedale Avenue
Mill Valley, CA 94941
(415) 383-6060
Fax: (415) 383-2520
e-mail: programs@csassociates.com

Curb Entertainment International
    Corp.
3907 West Alameda Avenue, Suite
    102
Burbank CA 91505
(818) 843-8580
Fax: (818) 566-1719

Darino Films
222 Park Avenue South
New York NY 10003
(212) 228-4024
Fax: (212) 228-3767

Devillier Donegan Enterprises
4401 Connecticut Avenue, NW
Washington, DC 20008
(202) 686-3980
Fax: (202) 686-3999

Direct Cinema, Ltd.
P.O. Box 10003
Santa Monica CA 90410
(310) 396-4774
Fax: (310) 396-3233
e-mail: directcinema@attmail.com

Distant Horizon Corporaion
8282 Sunset Blvd.
Los Angeles CA 90046
(213) 848-4140
Fax: (213) 848-4144

DMS Export Import
1540 North Highland, Ste. 110
Hollywood CA 90028
(213) 466-0121
Fax: (213) 466-0515

Dream Entertainment
8489 West 3rd Street, Suite 1096
Los Angeles CA 90048
(213) 655-5501
Fax: (213) 655-5603

Drift Releasing
611 Broadway, Suite 742
New York NY 10012
(212) 254-4118
Fax: (212) 254-3154

Educational Productions, Inc.
7412 SW Beaverton Hillsdale
   Highway, Suite 210
Portland OR 97725
(503) 292-9234/(800) 950-4949
Fax: (503) 292-9246

Educational Video Center
352 Park Avenue South, 4th Floor
New York NY 10010
(212) 725-3534
Fax: (212) 725-6501

The Educational Video Group
242 Southwind Way
Greenwood IN 46142
(317) 888-6581
Fax: (317) 881-5857
e-mail: 75047.620
   @compuserve.com

Electronic Arts Intermix
536 Broadway, 9th Floor
New York NY 10012
(212) 966-4605
Fax: (212) 941-6118

Entertainment Studios, Inc.
9830 Mohrs Cove Lane
Windermere FL 34786
(407) 291-8965
Fax: (407) 291-8988

Environmental Media Corporation
P.O. Box 1016
Chapel Hill NC 27514
(919) 933-3003
Fax: (919) 942-8785

ETR Associates
P.O. Box 1830
Santa Cruz CA 95061
(408) 438-4080 x238
Fax: (408) 438-4284

Expanded Entertainment
28024 Dorothy Drive
Agoura Hills CA 91301
(818) 991-2884
Fax: (818) 991-3773

Facets Multimedia, Inc.
1517 West Fullerton Ave.
Chicago, IL 60614
(312) 281-9075
Fax: (312) 929-5437

Fanlight Productions
47 Halifax Street
Boston MA 02130
(617) 937-4113
Fax: (617) 524-8838

Film Ideas, Inc.
3710 Commercial Avenue, Suite 13
Northbrook IL 60062
(800) 475-3456
Fax: (708) 480-7496

FilmHaus
2255 West Sepulveda Blvd., Suite
  204
Torrance CA 90501
(310) 320-8383
Fax: (310) 320-8384

Film-Makers' Cooperative
175 Lexington Avenue
New York, NY 10016
(212) 889-3820

Filmmakers Library
124 East 40th Street
New York NY 10016
(212) 808-4980
Fax: (212) 808-4983

Filmopolis Pictures
11300 W. Olympic Blvd., Suite 840
Los Angeles CA 90064
(310) 914-1776
Fax: (310) 914-1777

Films Around the World/
  Filmworld Television, Inc.
342 Madison Avenue, Suite 812
New York NY 10173
(212) 599-9500
Fax: (212) 599-6040
e-mail: alexjr@pipeline.com

Films for Educators, Inc./Films for
  Television
420 East 55th Street, Suite 6U
New York, NY 10022
(212) 486-6577
Fax: (212) 980-9826

Films for the Humanities and
  Sciences, Inc.®
P.O. Box 2053
Princeton NJ 08543-2053
(800) 257-5126/(609) 275-1400
Fax: (609) 275-3767

First Look Pictures Releasing
8800 Sunset Blvd., #302
Los Angeles CA 90069
(310) 855-1199
Fax: (310) 855-0719

First Run Features and First
  Run/Icarus
153 Waverly Place, 6th Floor
New York NY 10014
(212) 243-0600/(800) 876-1710
Fax: (212) 989-7649

Flower Films and Video
10341 San Pablo Avenue
El Cerrito, CA
(510) 525-0942

Fox Lorber Associates, Inc.
419 Park Avenue South, 20th Floor
New York NY 10016
(212) 686-6777
Fax: (212) 685-2625

Fox Searchlight Pictures
10201 West Pico Blvd.
Building 38, Room 110
Los Angeles CA 90035
(310) 369-2011
Fax: (310) 369-2359

Frameline Distribution
346 Ninth Street
San Francisco CA 94103
(415) 703-8654
Fax: (415) 861-1404
e-mail: frameline@aol.com

Fries Distribution Company
6922 Hollywood Boulevard
Los Angeles, CA 90028
(213) 466-2266

Glenn Photo Supply/Glenn Video
   Vistas, Ltd.
6924 Canby Avenue, Suite 103
Reseda CA 91355
(818) 881-8110
Fax: (818) 981-5506

Samuel Goldwyn Company
10203 Santa Monica Blvd.
Los Angeles CA 90067
(310) 552-2255
Fax: (310) 284-8493

GPN/University of Nebraska
PO Box 80669
Lincoln, NE 68501-0669
(800) 228-4630
Fax: (402) 472-4076
e-mail: gpn@unl.edu

Gramercy Pictures
9247 Alden Drive
Beverly Hills, CA 90210-3730
(310) 777-1960

Greycat Films
3829 Delaware Lane
Las Vegas NV 89109
(702) 737-0670
Fax: (702) 734-3628
e-mail: greycat@aol.com

Guidance Associates
90 South Bedford Road
Mt. Kisco NY 10549
(914) 666-4100
Fax: (914) 666-0172

Hemdale Entertainment
7966 Beverly Boulevard
Los Angeles, CA 90048-4512
(213) 966-3700
Fax: (213) 966-3750

Home Film Festival
P.O. Box 2032
Scranton PA 18501
(800) 258-3456
Fax: (717) 344-3810

Human Relations Media
175 Tomkins Avenue
Pleasantville NY 10570
(914) 769-6900
Fax: (914) 747-0839

Independent Video Services
401 East 10th Avenue, Suite 160
Eugene OR 97401-3317
(503) 345-3455
Fax: (503) 345-5951

Interama Video Classics
301 West 53rd Street, Suite 19E
New York, NY 10019
(212) 977-4830
Fax: (212) 581-6582

Intermedia
1300 Dexter Avenue North
Seattle WA 98109
(800) 553-8336
Fax: (206) 283-0778
e-mail: Shoff@lx.netcom.com

International Creative Exchange
3575 Cahuenga Blvd. West,
   Suite 475
Hollywood CA 90068
(213) 850-8080
Fax: (213) 850-8082

International Film Circuit
PO Box 1151
Old Chelsea Station
New York, NY 10011
(212) 779-0660
Fax: (212) 779-9129

International Film Foundation
155 West 72nd Street
New York, NY 10023
(212) 580-1111

International Video Network
2246 Camino Ramon
San Ramon CA 94583
(510) 866-1344 x245
Fax: (510) 866-9262

IRS Film Releasing
3520 Hayden Avenue
Culver City, CA 90232
(310) 838-7800
Fax: (310) 838-7402

ISA Releasing, Ltd.
680 North Lake Shore Drive, #1328
Chicago IL 60611
(312) 266-5900
Fax: (312) 266-1287

Italtoons Corporation
32 West 40th Street, Suite 2L
New York NY 10018
(212) 730-0280
Fax: (212) 730-0313

ITC Entertainment Group
12711 Ventura Boulevard
Studio City, CA 91604
(818) 760-2110
Fax: (818) 506-8189

Ivy Film and Video
P.O. Box 18376
Asheville, NC 28814
(704) 285-9995
Fax: (704) 285-9997
e-mail: joshtager@aol.com

Kino International Corporation
333 West 39th Street, Suite 503
New York NY 10018
(212) 629-6880
Fax: (212) 714) 714-0871

The Kitchen Video Distribution
   Collection
512 West 19th Street
New York, NY 10011
(212) 255-5793
Fax: (212) 645-4258
e-mail: Kitchen@panix.com
WWW: http://www.panix.com/
   kitchen.

KJM3 Entertainment Group, Inc.
274 Madison Avenue, Suite 601
New York NY 10016
(212) 689-0950
Fax: (212) 689-6861
e-mail: KJM3274@aol.com

Landmark Media
3450 Slade Run Drive
Falls Church VA 22042
(703) 241-2030/(800) 342-4336
Fax: (703) 536-9540

Leo Film Releasing
1509 N. Hoover, #1-2
Los Angeles CA 90027
(213) 913-3038
Fax: (213) 913-3038
e-mail: lustgarten@delphi.com

Live Entertainment
15400 Sherman Way
Van Nuys, CA 91406-4211
(818) 908-0303
Fax: (818) 778-3291

Lucerne Media
37 Ground Pine Road
Morris Plains NJ 07950
(201) 538-1401/(800) 341-2293
Fax: (201) 538-0855

Manbeck Pictures Corporation
3621 Wakonda Drive
Des Moines IA 50321-2132
(515) 285-1166

Maryknoll World Productions
Gonzaga Building
Maryknoll, NY 10545
(914) 941-7590
Fax: (914) 762-0316

MCA/Universal Home Video
70 Universal City Plaza
Universal City CA 91608
(818) 777-4300
Fax: (818) 733-1483

Medfilms, Inc.
6841 N. Cassim Place
Tucson AZ 85704
(602) 797-0345
Fax: (602) 742-6052

Media Guild
11722 Sorrento Valley Road, Suite E
San Diego CA 92121
(619) 755-9191/(800) 886-9196
Fax: (619) 755-4931

Media Methods
24097 North Shore Drive
Edwardsburg MI 49112
(616) 699-7061
Fax: (616) 699-7061
e-mail: Jmeuninck@aol.com

Merrimack Films
22D Hollywood Avenue
Ho-Ho-Kus NJ 07423
(201) 652-1989
Fax: (201) 652-1973

Milestone Film and Video, Inc.
275 West 96th Street, Suite 28C
New York, NY 10025
(212) 865-7449
Fax: (212) 222-8952
e-mail: MileFilms@aol.com

Miramax Films
375 Greenwich Street
New York NY 10013
(212) 941-3800
Fax: (212) 941-3949

MLR Films International
301 East 62nd Street
New York NY 10021
(212) 759-1729
Fax: (212) 759-8375

Arthur Mokin Productions, Inc.
P.O. Box 232
Santa Rosa CA 95402
(707) 542-4868
Fax: (707) 542-6182

Multimedia Entertainment, Inc.
45 Rockefeller Plaza, 35th Floor
New York NY 10111
(212) 332-2000
Fax: (212) 332-2010

Museum of Modern Art-Circulating
Film and Video Library
11 West 53rd Street
New York, NY 10019
(212) 708-9530
Fax: (212) 708-9531

Mypheduh Films, Inc.
403 K Street, NW
Washington DC 20001
(202) 289-6677
Fax: (202) 289-4477

Myriad Pictures
8899 Beverly Blvd., Suite 909
Los Angeles CA 90048
(310) 550-7588
Fax: (310) 550-1009

Mystic Fire Video
P.O. Box 422
New York, NY 10012-0008
(800) 999-1319/(212) 941-0999
Fax: (212) 941-1443
e-mail: mysticfire@echonyc.com
WWW: http://www.mysticfire.com/
~mysticfire

NAATA/Cross Current Media
National Asian American
Telecommunications Association
346 Ninth Street, 2nd Floor
San Francisco CA 94103
(415) 552-9550
Fax: (415) 863-7428

National Black Programming
Consortium
929 Harrison Avenue, Suite 101
Columbus, OH 43215
(614) 299-5355
Fax: (614) 299-4761

National Geographic Television
1145 17th Street, NW
Washington, DC 20036-4688
(202) 857-7680
Fax: (202) 775-6590

New and Unique Videos
2336 Sumac Drive
San Diego CA 92105
(619) 282-6126
Fax: (619) 283-8264
e-mail: videoduo@aol.com

New Day Films
22D Hollywood Avenue
Ho-Ho-Kus NJ 07423
(201) 652-6590
Fax: (201) 652-1973

New Dimension Media Inc.
85803 Lorane Highway
Eugene OR 97405
(503) 484-7125
Fax: (503) 485-5267

New Line Cinema
888 Seventh Avenue, 20th Floor
New York NY 10106
(212) 649-4900
Fax: (212) 649-4966

New Yorker Films
16 West 61st Street
New York NY 10023
(212) 247-6110
Fax: (212) 307-7855

Niteclub Video/Oddball Film and
    Video P.O. Box 425481
San Francisco CA 94142-5481
(415) 558-8112
Fax: (415) 863-9771

Northern Arts Entertainment, Inc.
Northern Arts Studios
Williamsburg MA 01096 (413) 268-
    9301
Fax: (413) 268-9309

October Films
65 Bleecker Street, 2nd Floor
New York NY 10012
(212) 539-4000
Fax: (212) 539-4099

Original Cinema
419 Park Avenue South, 20th floor
New York NY 10016
(212) 545-0177
Fax: (212) 685-2625

Orion Pictures – Classic Division
1888 Century Park East
Los Angeles CA 90272
(310) 282-0550
Fax: (310) 282-9902

Outsider Enterprises
2940 16th Street, Suite 200-1
San Francisco CA 94103
(415) 863-0611
Fax: (415) 863-0611

Overseas Filmgroup
8800 Sunset Blvd., Suite 302
Los Angeles CA 90069
(310) 855-1199
Fax: (310) 855-0719

Pacific Islanders in Communications
1221 Kapiolani Boulevard, #6A-4
Honolulu, HI 96814
(808) 591-0059
Fax: (808) 591-1114
e-mail: piccom@elele.peacesat.
    hawaii.edu

Panorama Entertainment
    Corporation
125 North Main Street
Port Chester NY 10573
(914) 937-1603
Fax: (914) 937-8496

Paper Tiger Television
339 Lafayette Street
New York, NY 10012
(212) 420-9045
Fax: (212) 420-8223
WWW: http://flicker.com/orgs/
    papertiger

Parabola Arts Foundation
656 Broadway
New York, NY 10012-2317
(800) 560-MYTH
Fax: (212) 979-7325

Kit Parker Films
P.O. Box 16022
Monterey CA 93942
(408) 393-0303
Fax: (408) 393-0304

Passport Cinemas, Ltd.
2 Yates Street
Albany NY 12208
(518) 453-1000
Fax: (518) 453-1350

Pathe News, Inc./Pathe Pictures, Inc.
270 Madison Avenue, 5th floor
New York, NY 10019
(212) 696-0392

PBS Video
1320 Braddock Place
Alexandria, VA 22314-1698
(703) 739-5000
Fax: (703) 739-0775

Phoenix Films and Video
2349 Chaffee Drive
St. Louis MO 63146
(314) 569-0211
Fax: (314) 569-2834

Picture Start, Inc.
1727 W. Catalpa Avenue
Chicago IL 60640-1105
(312) 769-2489
Fax: (312) 769-4467

Premier Studios
3033 Locust Street
St. Louis MO 63103
(314) 531-3555
Fax: (314) 531-9588

Public Media Home Video/Public
  Media Education
5547 North Ravenswood Avenue
Chicago IL 60640-1199
(312) 878-2600
Fax: (312) 878-8406

Pyramid Film and Video
2801 Colorado Avenue
Santa Monica CA 90406
(310) 828-7577/(800) 421-2304
Fax: (310) 453-9083

Rainbow Releasing
9165 Sunset Blvd., Suite 300
Los Angeles CA 90069
(310) 271-0202
(310) 271-2753

Raven Pictures International
859 Hollywood Way, Suite 273
Burbank CA 91505
(818) 508-4785
Fax: (818) 508-4786

Reel Movies International
8235 Douglas Avenue, Suite 770
Dallas TX 75225
(214) 363-4400
Fax: (214) 739-3456

Republic Pictures
5700 Wilshire Blvd., #525
Los Angeles CA 90036
(310) 965-6900

Rhapsody Films, Inc.
P.O. Box 179
10 Charlton Street
New York NY 10014
(212) 243-0152
Fax: (212) 645-9250

Rigel Independent Distribution and
  Entertainment
2338 San Marco Drive
Los Angeles CA 90068
(213) 467-0240
Fax: (213) 467-1679

RKO Pictures
1801 Avenue of the Stars
Los Angeles, CA 90067
(310) 277-0707
Fax: (310) 284-8574

Roxie Releasing
3125 16th Street
San Francisco CA 94103
(415) 431-3611
(415) 431-2822

Savoy Pictures
2425 Olympic Blvd., 6th Floor
Santa Monica CA 90404
(310) 247-7329
Fax: (310) 247-7239

Select Media, Inc.
225 Lafayette Street, Suite 1002
New York NY 10012
(212) 431-8923
Fax: (212) 431-8946

Seventh Art Releasing
7551 Sunset Blvd., #104
Los Angeles CA 90046
(213) 845-1455
Fax: (213) 845-4717

Shadow Distribution
P.O. Box 1246
Waterville ME 04903
(207) 872-5111
Fax: (207) 872-5502

Silverstein International Corporation
171 West 57th Street, Suite 12B
New York, NY 10019
(212) 541-6620
Fax: (212) 586-0085

Sony Pictures Classics, Inc.
550 Madison Avenue
New York NY 10022
(212) 833-8833
Fax: (212) 833-8844

Strand Releasing
225 Santa Monica Blvd., Suite 810
Santa Monica CA 90401
(310) 395-5002
Fax: (310) 395-2502

Sunburst Communications, Inc.
39 Washington Avenue
Pleasantville NY 10570
(914) 769-5030/(800) 431-1934
Fax: (914) 769-5211

Swank Motion Pictures
350 Vanderbilt Motor Parkway
Hauppauge, NY 11781-4305
(516) 434-1560
Fax: (516) 434-1574
910 Riverside Drive
Elmhurst, IL 60126-4967
(708) 833-0061
Fax: (708) 833-0096
201 S. Jefferson Avenue
St. Louis, MO 63103-2579
(314) 534-6300
Fax: (314) 289-2192

Tapestry International, Ltd.
920 Broadway, Suite 1501
New York NY 10010
(212) 505-2288
Fax: (212) 505-5059

Tapeworm Video Distributors
12420 Montague Street
Arleta CA 91331
(818) 896-8899
Fax: (818) 896-3855

Tara Releasing
124 Belvedere Street
San Rafael, CA 94901-4707
(415) 454-5838

Taurus Entertainment Company
Sunset Gower Studios
1420 N. Beachwood Drive
Box 2, Bldg. 50
Hollywood CA 90028
(213) 993-7355
Fax: (213) 993-7316

Chip Taylor Communications
15 Spollett Drive
Derry NH 03038
(603) 434-9262
Fax: (603) 434-9262
e-mail: chiptaylor@delphi.com

Third World Newsreel
335 West 38th Street, 5th Floor
New York NY 10018
(212) 947-9277
Fax: (212) 594-6417

Transcontinental Pictures Industries
650 North Bronson Avenue
Hollywood CA 90004
(213) 464-2279
Fax: (213) 464-3212

Trident Releasing
8401 Melrose Place, 2nd Floor
Los Angeles CA 90069
(213) 655-8818
Fax: (213) 655-0515

Trimark Pictures
2644 30th Street
Santa Monica CA 90405
(310) 314-2000
Fax: (310) 452-9614

Triumph Films
10202 West Washington Blvd.
Culver City CA 90232
(310) 280-4036
Fax: (310) 280-4988

Troma, Inc.
1501 Broadway, #2605
New York, NY 10036
(212) 997-0595
Fax: (212) 997-0968

United Learning, Inc.
6633 West Howard Street
Niles IL 60648
(708) 647-0600
Fax: (708) 647-0918

United Nations Audio Visual
Promotion and Distribution
Dept. of Public Information, Media
Division, Room S-805A
United Nations
New York NY 10017
(212) 963-6982
Fax: (212) 963-6869
e-mail: sue-ting-len@un.org.

University of California Extension
Center for Media and
Independent Learning
2000 Center Street, 4th Floor
Berkeley CA 94704
(510) 642-0460
Fax: (510) 643-9271
e-mail: dbickley@uclink.berkeley.edu

Upstate Films
P.O. Box 324
Rhinebeck NY 12572
(914) 876-4546
Fax: (914) 876-2353

Video Data Bank
School of the Art Institute of Chicago
37 S. Wabash
Chicago IL 60603
(312) 345-3550
Fax: (312) 541-8073

Videodisc Publishing, Inc./VPI/AC
Video, Inc.
381 Park Ave South, Suite 620
New York, NY 10016
212) 685-5522
Fax: (212) 685-5482

The Video Project
5332 College Avenue, Suite 101
Oakland CA 94168
(415) 655-9050
Fax: (415) 655-9115

Vision Makers Video
Native American Public Broadcasting
   Consortium
PO Box 83111
Lincoln, NE 68501
(402) 472-3522

Vision Video/Gateway Films, Inc.
P.O. Box 540
2030 Wentz Church Road
Worcester PA 19490
(215) 584-1893
Fax: (215) 584-4610
e-mail: visionvide@aol.com

Vista Street Entertainment
9911 West Pico Blvd., Suite PH-P
Los Angeles CA 90035
(310) 556-3074
Fax: (310) 556-8815

Vocational Marketing Services (VMS)
17600 South Williams Street, #6
Thornton IL 60476
(708) 877-2814
Fax: (708) 877-2819

Warner Home Video
4000 Warner Blvd.
Burbank, CA 91522
(818) 954-6429
Fax: (818) 954-6540

Women Make Movies
462 Broadway
New York NY 10013
(212) 925-0606
Fax: (212) 925-2052

World Wide Pictures, Inc.
1201 Hennepin Avenue
Minneapolis MN 55459
(612) 338-3335
Fax: (612) 338-3029

Zeitgeist Films, Ltd.
247 Centre Street, 2nd Floor
New York NY 10013
(212) 274-1989
Fax: (212) 274-1644
e-mail: zeitgeist@tunanet.com

Zenger Media
10,200 Jefferson Blvd.
Culver City CA 90232
(310) 839-2436/(800) 421-4246

The following companies were listed in the previous edition of the **AIVF Guide to Film and Video Distributors.** We have listed the last available information. Since surveys mailed to these companies were not returned as undeliverable, several companies may still be in business, may have moved, changed names, or merged with other companies.

Academic Media Service
University of Colorado Media Center
Campus Box 379
Boulder, CO 80309
(403) 255-2655

Academy Entertainment
1 Pine Haven Shore Road
Shelburne, VT 05842
(802) 985-2060
Fax: (802) 985-3403

ACI
6100 Wilshire Blvd.
Los Angeles, CA 90048
(213) 932-6100
Fax: (213) 932-6960

Agency for Instructional Technology
1111 West 17th Street
Bloomington, IN 47401
(812) 339-2203

A.I.P. Distribution
10726 McCune Avenue
Los Angeles, CA 90034
(213) 559-8805
Fax: (213) 559-8849

Alice Communications, Ltd./Alice
    Entertainment, Inc.
23632 Calabasas Road, Suite 107B
Calabasas, CA 91302
(805) 688-1523

Alliance Entertainment
8439 Sunset Blvd., Suite 404
Los Angeles, CA 90069
(213) 654-9488
Fax: (213) 654-9786

American Cinema Marketing
    Corporation
3575 Cahuenga Blvd. West, Suite
    455
Los Angeles, CA 90068
(213) 850-6400
Fax: (213) 850-7117

Aquarius Releasing, Inc.
630 Ninth Avenue, Suite 908
New York, NY 10036
(212) 245-8530

Art Com
P.O. Box 3123 Rincon Annex
San Francisco, CA 94119-3123
(415) 431-7524
Fax: (415) 431-7841

Audio Vision
3 Morningside Place
Norwalk, CT 06854
(203) 838-9225

August Entertainment
838 North Fairfax Avenue
Los Angeles, CA 90046
(213) 658-8888
Fax: (213) 466-7654

Baker and Taylor Video
501 South Gladiolus
Momence, IL 60954

Benchmark Films, Inc.
145 Scarborough Road
Briarcliff Manor, NY 10510
(914) 762-3838
Fax: (914) 3895

Blue Ridge Entertainment
10490 Santa Monica Blvd.
Los Angeles, CA 90025
(310) 474-6688
Fax: (310) 475-2677

Camera One
431-A North 34th Street
Seattle, WA 98103
(206) 547-5131

Capella International, Inc.
9242 Beverly Blvd., Suite 280
Beverly Hills, CA 90210-3710
(310) 247-4700
Fax: (310) 247-4701

Capitol Entertainment
P.O. Box 2803
Washington, DC 20013
(202) 636-9203

Caridi Video
250 West 57th Street, Suite 811
New York, NY 10107
(212) 581-2277
Fax: (212) 581-2278

CBC Enterprises
350 Fifth Avenue, Suite 35507
New York, NY 10118
(212) 760-1500

Centre Communications
1800 30th Street, Suite 207
Boulder, CO 80301
(303) 444-1166
Fax: (303) 444-1168

Cinema Concepts, Inc.
2461 Berlin Turnpike
Newington, CT 06111

Cinematic Releasing Corporation
P.O. Box 106
Demarest, NJ07627
(201) 784-0662

Cinephile/Aurora Releasing
306 West 38th Street, Suite 603
New York, NY 10018
(212) 947-1334

CineTel Films
3800 West Alameda Ave., Suite 825
Burbank, CA91505
(818) 955-9551
Fax: (818) 955-9616

Cinetrust Entertainment Corporation
2121 Avenue of the Stars, 6th Floor
Los Angeles, CA 90067
(213) 551-6504
Fax: (213) 551-6622

Cobra Entertainment Group
16530 Ventura Blvd., Suite 308
Encino, CA 91436
(818) 981-0223
Fax: (818) 981-0221

Cori Films International
2049 Century Park East, Suite 780
Los Angeles, CA 90067
(213) 557-0173
Fax: (213) 551-4974

Cornet/MTI Films and Video
108 Wilmot Road
Deerfield, IL 60015
(708) 940-1260/(800-621-2131
Fax: (708) 940-3600

Creative Film Society
8435 Geyser Avenue
Northridge, CA 91324
(818) 885-7288

Crown International Pictures, Inc.
8701 Wilshire Blvd.
Beverly Hills, CA 90211
(213) 657-6700
Fax: (213) 657-4489

Davis Panzer Productions
1438 North Gower Street, Suite 401
Hollywood, CA 90028
(213) 463-2343
Fax: (213) 465-0948

Walt Disney Educational Media
    Company
500 South Buena Vista Street
Burbank, CA 91521
(818) 560-1000

Documentaries for Learning
74 Fenwood Road
Boston, MA 02115
(617) 926-0491
Fax: (617) 926-9519

Education Development Center
55 Chapel Street
Newton, MA02160
(617) 969-7100

Educational Technology Corporation
Box 5069
Appleton, WI85106
(414) 735-0701

Embassy Films
1438 North Gower, Box 27
Los Angeles, CA 90028
(213) 460-7200
Fax: (213) 881-8110

Encyclopedia Britannica Education
    Corporation
310 North Michigan Avenue
Chicago, IL 60604
(312) 347-7966

Epic Productions
1551 North La Brea
Los Angeles, CA 90028
(213) 850-6110
Fax: (213) 850-0787

Ergo Media, Inc.
P.O. Box 2037
Teaneck, NJ 07666
(201) 692-0404
Fax: (201) 692-0663

Euramco International Inc.
9430 West Washington Blvd., Suite 7
Culver City, CA 90230
(213) 204-4801

EZTV
8547 Santa Monica Blvd.
West Hollywood, CA 90069
(213) 657-1532

Falcon Arts and Entertainment, Inc.
12190 1/2 Ventura Blvd., Suite
    2200
Studio City, CA 91064
(818) 985-6341
Fax: (818) 762-7901

Family Films
3558 South Jefferson Avenue
St. Louis, MO 63118
(314) 664-7000

Festival Films
2841 Irving Avenue South
Minneapolis, MN 55408
(612) 870-4744

Film Communicators
4314 Mariot Avenue
North Hollywood, CA 91601
(818) 766-3747

Film Wright
4530 18th Street
San Francisco, CA 94114
(415) 863-6100

Filmstar Inc.
12301 Wilshire Blvd., Suite 505
Los Angeles, CA 90025
(213) 207-6331
Fax: (213) 207-3195

Filmtrust Motion Picture
    Licensing, Inc.
10490 Santa Monica Blvd.
Los Angeles, CA 90025
(213) 474-6688
Fax: (213) 475-2677

Film/World Distributors, Inc.
342 Madison Avenue
New York, NY 10173
(212) 599-9500
Fax: (212) 59-6040

First American Films
368 East Pershing Drive
Playa Del Ray, CA 90293
(213) 822-0178

Gaga Communications
1888 Century Park East, Suite 1000
Los Angeles, CA 90067
(213) 556-1993
Fax: (213) 556-3165

Gibraltar Releasing Organization
14101 Valleyheart Drive, Suite 205
Sherman Oaks, CA 91424
(818) 501-2076
Fax: (818) 501-5138

Green Mountain Post Films
P.O. Box 229
Turner's Falls, MA 01376
(413) 863-4754/863-8248

Group I Films
9230 Robin Drive
Los Angeles, CA 90069
(213) 550-7280

Harmony Vision
116 North Robertson Blvd.
Los Angeles, CA 90046
(213) 652-8844

Hartley Film Foundation
59 Cat Rock Road
Cos Cob, CT 06807
(203) 869-1818

Hollywood Home Theater
1540 North Highland Avenue
Los Angeles, CA 90029
(213) 466-0121

Home Vision
P.O. Box 800
Concord, MA01742
(800) 262-8600

Hurlock Cine-World, Inc.
P.O. Box 34619
Juneau, AK 99803-4619
(907) 637-4319

Image Organization
9000 Sunset Blvd., Suite 915
Los Angeles, CA 90069
(213) 278-8751
Fax: (213) 278-3967

Impact Filmgroup
9014 Ashcroft Avenue
West Hollywood, CA 90048
(213) 855-1199

Imperial Entertainment Corporation
4640 Lankershim Blvd., 4th Floor
North Hollywood, CA 91602
(818) 762-0005
Fax: (818) 762-0006

Independent Network, Inc./Film
  Ventures International, Inc.
11150 Olympic Blvd., Suite 1100
Los Angeles, CA 90064
(213) 479-6755
Fax: (213) 479-3475

Indiana University Audiovisual
  Center
Bloomington, IN 47405-5901
(812) 855-8087
Fax: (812) 855-8404

Ingram Entertainment
347 Reedwood Drive
Nashville, TN 37217
(800) 759-5000

Inter-Ocean Film Sales, Ltd.
6100 Wilshire Blvd., Suite 1500
Los Angeles, CA 90048
(213) 932-0500
Fax: (213) 932-0238

International Film Bureau
332 South Michigan Avenue
Chicago, IL 60604-4382
(312) 427-4545

International Film Marketing, Inc.
9440 Santa Monica Blvd., Suite 707
Beverly Hills, CA 90210
(213) 273-4208
Fax: (213) 276-8950

International Historic Films
Box 29035
Chicago, IL 60629
(312) 927-2900

International Media Services
718 Sherman Avenue
Plainfield, NJ 07060
(201) 756-4060

International Video Entertainment,
  Inc. (IVE)
15400 Sherman Way, Suite 500
Van Nuys, CA 91410-0124
(818) 908-0303
Fax: (818) 908-0320

Intertrade Film Distributors
959 North Seward Street
Hollywood, CA 90038
(213) 464-7622
Fax: (213) 464-6557

ITC Entertainment Group
12711 Ventura Blvd., Suite 440
Studio City, CA 91604
(818) 760-2110
Fax: (818) 506-8189

J&M Entertainment
1289 Sunset Plaza Drive
Los Angeles, CA 90069
(213) 652-7733

Janson Associates, Inc.
560 Sylvan Avenue
Englewood Cliffs, NJ 07632
(201) 568-0809
Fax: (201) 568-2153

Karol Media
22 Riverview Drive
Wayne, NJ 07470
(201) 628-9111

Kings Road Entertainment
1901 Avenue of the Stars, Suite 605
Los Angeles, CA 90067
(213) 552-0057
Fax: (213) 277-4468

Kodiak Films, Inc.
11075 Santa Monica Blvd.
Los Angeles, CA 90025
(213) 479-8575

K.R.G. Film Sales
1901 Avenue of the Stars, Suite 605
Los Angeles, CA 90067
(213) 552-0057

Kultur Video
121 Highway #36
West Long Branch, NJ 07764
(201) 229-2343
Fax: (201) 229-0066

Little Red Filmhouse
119 South Kilkea Drive
Los Angeles, CA 90048
(213) 653-0407

Lorimar Home Video
4000 Warner Blvd., Bldg. 154,
    Room 322
Burbank, CA 91522
(818) 954-6000

Magder ADN Pictures
111 Great Neck Road, Suite 604
Great Neck, NY 11201
(516) 487-6640

Marketing International, Inc.
95 Commerce
Stamford, CT06902
(203) 323-2999

Marquee Entertainment
9044 Melrose Ave.
Los Angeles, CA 90061

Mass Media Ministries
2116 North Charles Street
Baltimore, MD 21218
(301) 727-3270

McDonagh-Davis Associates, Inc.
1256 Sulphur Spring Rd.
Baltimore, MD 21227
(410) 536-1964
Fax: (410) 536-8136

M.C.E.G. International/Manson
    International/Virgin Vision Ltd.
2400 Broadway, Suite 100
Santa Monica, CA 90404
(213) 208-8899
Fax: (213) 208-8899

Media Design Associates, Inc./West
    Wind Productions, Inc.
P.O. Box 3189
Boulder, CO 80307
(303) 443-2800

Media Exchange
217 South Payne Street
Alexandria, VA 22314
(703) 548-7039

Media Home Entertainment, Inc.
5730 Buckingham Parkway
Culver City, CA 90230
(213) 216-7900/(800) 421-4509
Fax: (213) 216) 9305

Media, Inc.
P.O. Box 496
Media, PA 19063
(215) 565-2844

Media Ventures Organization
6350 Laurel Canyon Blvd., Suite 416
North Hollywood, CA 91606
(818) 761-6516
Fax: (213) 852-4926

Miracle Films
6311 Romaine Street, Suite 7305
Los Angeles, CA 90038
(213) 466-0676

Modern Talking Picture Servcie
5000 Park Street North
St. Petersburg, FL 33709
(813) 541-5763
Fax: (813) 546-0681

Modern Visual Communications
9016 Wilshire Blvd., Suite 220
Beverly Hills, CA 90211
(213) 659-7439

Monterey Movie Company
5142 North Clareton Street,
    Suite 270
Agoura Hills, CA 91301
(818) 597-0047
Fax: (818) 597-0105

Moonstone Entertainment
9242 Beverly Blvd., Suite 230
Beverly Hills, CA 90210-3710
(310) 247-6060
Fax: (310) 247-6061

Morgan Creek International
1875 Century Park East, Suite 200
Los Angeles, CA 90067
(213) 284-8884
Fax: (213) 282-8794

Morris Video
2730 Monterey Street, Suite 105
Torrance, CA90503
(213) 533-4800

Movie Craft Entertainment
12 Moray Court
Baltimore, MD 21236
(301) 256-5909

The Movie Group
1900 Avenue of the Stars,
    Suite 1425
Los Angeles, CA 90067
(213) 556-2830
Fax: (213) 277-1490

Moviestore Entertainment
11111 Santa Monica Blvd.,
    Suite 1850
Los Angeles, CA 90067
(213) 478-4230
Fax: (213) 478-2538

National Health Video Inc.
12021 Wilshire Blvd., Suite 550
Los Angeles, CA 90025
(213) 472-2275
Fax: (213) 312-9757

New Visions Pictures
5750 Wilshire Blvd., Suite 600
Los Angeles, CA 90036
(213) 965-2500
Fax: (213) 965-2599

NFL Films
330 Fellowship Road
Mt. Laurel, NJ 08054
(609) 778-1600

NSI Video
Box 895
Hermosa Beach, CA 90254
(213) 374-7476

Odyssey/Cinecom International
6500 Wilshire Blvd., Suite 400
Los Angeles, CA 90048
(213) 655-9335
Fax: (213) 655-1928

Omega Entertainment
8760 Shoreham Drive
Los Angeles, CA 90069
(213) 855-016
Fax: (213) 650-0325

OneWest Media
P.O. Box 5766
Santa Fe, NM87502-5766
(505) 983-8685
Fax: (505) 982-4757

Orbis Communications
8800 W. Sunset Blvd.
Los Angeles, CA 90069-2105
(212) 685-6699

Pacific International Enterprises, Inc.
P.O. Box 1727
1133 South Riverside, Suite 1
Medford, OR 97501
(503) 779-0990
Fax: (503) 779-8880

Pacific Motion Pictures
824 1/2 North Harper Ave.
Los Angeles, CA 90046
(213) 655-1684
Fax: (213) 655-3654

Palisades Wildlife Film Library
1205 South Ogden Drive
Los Angeles, CA 90019
(213) 931-6186

Pennsylvania State University
   AudioVisual Services
212 Special Services Bldg.
University Park, PA 16802
(814) 865-6314

Picturmedia Ltd.
119-45 Union Turnpike
Forest Hills, NY 11375
(718) 268-8646

PM Entertainment Group
16780 Schoenborn Street
Sepulveda, CA 91343
(818) 891-1288
Fax: (818) 892-8391

Praxis Media, Inc.
18 Marshal Street
South Norwalk, CT 06854
(203) 866-6666

Premiere Film Marketing
6464 Sunset Blvd., Penthouse 1130
Hollywood, CA 90028
(213) 962-4950
Fax: (213) 962-8922

Prism Entertainment
1888 Century Park East, Suite 1000
Los Angeles, CA 90067
(213) 277-3270
Fax: (213) 203-8036

Professional Media Service
   Corporation
13620 South Crenshaw Blvd.
Gardena, CA 90249
(213) 532-9024
Fax: (213) 532-0131

Program Source International
2494 Loch Creek Way
Bloomfield Hills, MI 48013
(313) 333-2010
Fax: (313) 333-2012

Quest Entertainment
P.O. Box 616626
Orlando, FL 32861
(407) 363-8440
Fax: (407) 363-8449

Questar Video Communications
P.O. Box 11345
Chicago, IL 60611
(312) 266-9400
Fax: (312) 266-9523

Radiance Films International
216 Main Street, Suite A
Venice, CA 90291
(213) 399-0095
Fax: (213) 396-6244

Research Press
2612 N. Mattis Avenue
Champaign, IL 61826
(217) 352-3273

Shapiro Glickenhaus Entertainment
12001 Ventura Place
Studio City, CA 91040
(818) 766-8500
Fax: (818) 766-7873

Signals
274 Fillmore Avenue East
St. Paul, MN 55107
(800) 733-2232

Silver Star Film Corporation
8833 West Sunset Blvd., Suite 406
Los Angeles, CA 90069
(213) 652-9290

Sterling Educational Films
241 Est 34th Street
New York, NY 10016

The Stutz Company
2600 Tenth Street
Berkeley, CA94701
(415) 644-2200
Fax: (415) 644-2230

Trans Atlantic Entertainment
1440 S. Sepulveda Blvd., Suite 118
Los Angeles, CA 90025
(310) 445-1381
Fax: (310) 445-1359

TMS Pictures, Inc.
11111 Santa Monica, Suite 1850
Los Angeles, CA 90025
(213) 478-4230
Fax: (213) 478-2538

Today Home Entertainment, Inc.
9200 Sunset Blvd.
Los Angeles, CA 90069
(213) 278-6490

Trans World Films, Inc.
332 South Michigan Avenue
Chicago, IL 60604
(312) 922-1530

TransWorld Entertainment
3330 West Cahuenga Blvd.,
    Suite 500
Los Angeles, CA 90068
(213) 969-2800
Fax: (213) 969-8352

Triton Entertainment Corporation
10746 Magnolia Blvd.
North Hollywood, CA 91601
(213) 877-4066

University of Illinois Film Center
1325 South Oak Street
Champaign, IL 61820
(800) 367-3456

Vantage Communications, Inc.
Box 546
78 Main Street
Nyack, NY 10960
(914) 358-0147

Varied Directions
69 Elm Street
Camden, ME 04843
(207) 236-8506

Videocassette Marketing Corporation
137 Eucalyptus Drive
El Segundo, CA 90245
(213) 322-1140

Videodiscovery
1700 Westlake Ave., N., Suite 600
Seattle, WA 98109-9245
(206) 285-5400
Fax: (206) 285-9245

VideoStar Connections, Inc.
3490 Piedmont Raod, N.E.
Atlanta, GA 30305
(404) 262-1555

Vidiots
302 Pico Blvd.
Santa Monica, CA 90405
(213) 392-8508

Vidmark International
2901 Ocean Park Blvd., Suite 123
Santa Monica, CA 90405
(213) 399-8877
Fax: (213) 399-3828

Vineyard Video Productions
Elias Lane
West Tisbury, MA 02575
(508) 693-3584

Virgin Vision
6100 Wilshire Blvd., 16th Floor
Los AngelesCA90048
(213) 315) 7800
Fax: (213) 315-7850

Vision International
3330 Cahuenga Blvd. West,
   Suite 500
Los Angeles, CA 90068
(213) 969-2900

Voyager
578 Broadway, Suite 406
New York, NY 10012
(212) 431-5199
Fax: (212) 431-5799

Weston Woods Studios, Inc.
389 Newtown Turnpike
Weston, CT 06883
(203) 226-3355/(800) 243-5020
Fax: (203) 226-3818

Wishing Well Distributing Company
P.O. Box 529
Graton, CA 95444
(707) 823-9355
Fax: (707) 829-7681

Women's Video Collective
P.O. Box 1609
Cambridge, MA 02238
(617) 492-2126

THE AIVF GUIDE TO FILM AND VIDEO DISTRIBUTORS

A Publication of the Foundation for Independent Video and Film, Inc.

TO: FILM AND VIDEO DISTRIBUTORS

RE: UPDATE FOR THE NEXT EDITION OF THE AIVF
GUIDE TO FILM AND VIDEO DISTRIBUTORS

As you may know, *The AIVF Guide To Film And Video Distributors* is updated every few years. We would like to make sure that we continue to have updated information for inclusion of your company in the next edition.

In order for us to have the most complete information about your company, we would appreciate it if you would take a moment to look over and complete the following questionnaire.

Please feel free to send any additional information (brochures, catalogs, etc.). Also, please be as descriptive as possible. The more information we have, the more accurate and thorough we can be.

Inclusion in the *Distributors Guide* will enhance the awareness of your company throughout the independent media community.

Please return to:

AIVF/FIVF
Distributors Guide Update
304 Hudson Street, 6th Floor
New York, NY 10013
(212) 807-1400
Fax: (212) 463-8519

Thank you so much for your attention and anticipated response.

THE AIVF GUIDE TO FILM AND VIDEO DISTRIBUTORS

GENERAL INFORMATION

Company Name _____

Address _____

City _____ State _____ Zip _____

Telephone _____ Fax _____ E-Mail _____

Company Officers _____

Number of Company Employees / Staff Size _____

Contact for Acquisitions _____

Year Established _____ Area of Specialty _____

COMPANY PROFILE

*Please feel free to attach additional comments which would
give a comprehensive picture of your company.*

- What types of films/videos/television programs does your company handle (e.g., feature, documentary/educational, video, specialty)? What are
  qualities you look for in productions which the company would be interested in acquiring?

  _____

  _____

  _____

- What are some examples of titles in your collection? (Current catalog,
  brochure or annual report would be useful.)

  _____

  _____

  _____

- How many titles are in your library? How many are currently being distributed?

  _____

- Will you look at works-in-progress or rough cuts?_____

- What kinds of deals is your company willing to make (e.g., negative pickups, advances/guarantees, etc.)?

  _____

- What are your company's primary methods of acquisition (e.g., festivals, markets, screenings, working with contract producers, submissions from independent producers, etc.)? What do you consider the most effective venues?

  _____

- Have you handled or will you handle work considered to be a risk— by unknown or younger directors, for example? _____

- What are your company's primary markets?
  ❏ Theatrical   ❏ Non-Theatrical   ❏ Semi-Theatrical   ❏ Home Video
  ❏ Other_____
  Television: ❏ Pay   ❏ Network   ❏ Public   ❏ Syndication
               ❏ Satellite   ❏ Cable
  Foreign Markets_____

- What should producers supply (e.g., prints, masters, publicity materials, etc.)?

  _____

- A brief description of your company would be very helpful:_____

  _____

  _____

  _____

  _____

Please return to: AIVF Guide to Film and Video Distributors
304 Hudson Street, 6th Floor, New York, NY 10013
(212) 807-1400   fax: (212) 463-8519

Distributor Report Card

Attention media makers: AIVF/FIVF is compiling information for a "consumer's bureau" on film and video distributors. Copy this form and return it to us with your feedback about distribution arrangements you've experienced. You may include your name or remain anonymous as you prefer, keeping in mind that **your submitted responses will be freely available to makers who are contemplating working with that distributor.** We may also use this information to alert distributors to ongoing or repeated complaints, so as to help them improve their relations with and services to makers. Return to: Distributors Bureau, AIVF/FIVF, 304 Hudson Street, 6th Floor, NYC 10013; fax (212) 463-8519.

Date submitted: _____

DISTRIBUTOR NAME: _____

LOCATION (incl. city and state/country): _____

_____

_____

Your Name: *(Optional)* _____

Title of work distributed: _____

Format _____ Length _____

Year(s) this report covers: _____

Use a grading system, with 1 representing the lowest grade through 6 as the highest.

FULFILLMENT OF PROMISES MADE BY DISTRIBUTOR REGARDING:

        Initial promotion _____

        Consistency of promotion _____

        Frequency of promotion _____

        Financial arrangements _____

        Other (specify) _____

_____

_____

_____

DID THE DISTRIBUTOR MEET YOUR EXPECTATIONS IN TERMS OF:

Income projection _____

Income reports _____

Promptness of payments to you _____

Other (specify) _____

_____

_____

CATALOG AND PROMOTION:

Location/prominence of your work in distribution catalog _____

Was your work treated with respect in the distributor's catalog? _____

Was your work treated accurately in the catalog? _____

Quality of information other than in distribution catalog _____

Other (specify): _____

_____

_____

HUMAN RELATIONS:

Distributor staff: _____

Respect for you? _____

Respect for your work? _____

Other (specify): _____

_____

_____

Was it worth it for you to have your work handled by this distributor? Y/N

Would you use this distributor again? Y/N

Overall distributor grade: _____

Note any other relevant experiences—positive or negative— with regard to this distributor (attach additional pages if necessary): _____

_____

_____

_____

THE ASSOCIATION OF
INDEPENDENT VIDEO & FILMMAKERS

Diverse, committed, opinionated, and fiercely independent—these are the video and filmmakers who are members of AIVF. Documentary and feature filmmakers, animators, experimentalists, distributors, educators, students, curators—all concerned that their work make a difference—find the Association of Independent Video and Filmmakers, the national service organization for independent producers, vital to their professional lives. Whether it's our magazine, *The Independent Film & Video Monthly,* or the organization raising its collective voice to advocate for important issues, AIVF preserves your independence while letting you know you're not alone.

AIVF helps you save time and money as well. You'll find you can spend more of your time (and less of your money) on what you do best—getting your work made and seen. To succeed as an independent today, you need a wealth of resources, strong connections, and the best information available. So join with more than 5,000 other independents who rely on AIVF to help them succeed.

JOIN AIVF TODAY!
Here's what membership offers:

THE INDEPENDENT FILM & VIDEO MONTHLY

Membership provides you with a year's subscription to *The Independent.* Thought-provoking features, news, and regular columns on business, technical, and legal matters. Plus festival listings, funding deadlines, exhibition venues, and announcements of member activities and new programs and services. Special issues highlight regional activity and focus on subjects including media education and the new technologies.

INSURANCE

Members are eligible to purchase discounted personal and production insurance plans through AIVF suppliers. A wide range of health insurance options are available, as well as special liability, E&O, and production plans tailored for the needs of low-budget mediamakers.

TRADE DISCOUNTS

A growing list of businesses across the country offer AIVF members discounts on equipment and auto rentals, film processing, transfers, editing, and other production necessities. Plus long-distance and overnight courier services are available at special rates for AIVF members from national companies. In New York, members receive discounted rates at two hotels to make attendance at our programs and other important events more convenient.

CONFERENCE/SCREENING ROOM

AIVF's new office has a low-cost facility for members to hold meetings and small private screenings of work for friends, distributors, programmers, funders, and producers.

INFORMATION

We distribute a series of publications on financing, funding, distribution, and production; members receive discounts on selected titles. AIVF's staff also can provide information about distributors, festivals, and general information pertinent to your needs. Our library houses information on everything from distributors to sample contracts to budgets.

WORKSHOPS, PANELS, AND SEMINARS

Members get discounts on events covering the whole spectrum of current issues and concerns affecting the field, ranging from business and aesthetic to technical and political topics. Plus: members-only evenings with festival directors, producers, distributors, cable programmers, and funders.

ADVOCACY

Members receive periodic advocacy alerts, with updates on important legislative issues affecting the independent field and mobilization for collective action.

COMMUNITY

AIVF sponsors monthly member get-togethers in cities across the country; call the office for the one nearest you. Plus members are carrying on active dialogue online—creating a "virtual community" for independents to share information, resources, and ideas. Another way to reach fellow independents to let them know about your screenings, business services, and other announcements is by renting our mailing list, available at a discount to members.

MEMBERSHIP CATEGORIES

Individual/Student Membership
Year's subscription to *The Independent* • Access to all plans and discounts • Festival/ Distribution/Library services • Information Services • Discounted admission to seminars • Book discounts • Advocacy action alerts • Eligibility to vote and run for board of directors

Supporting Membership
All the above for two individuals at one address, with 1 subscription to *The Independent*

Non-profit Organizational/Business & Industry Membership
All the above benefits, except access to health insurance plans • 2 copies of *The Independent* • 1 free FIVF-published book per year • Complimentary bulk shipments of *The Independent* to conferences, festivals, and other special events • Special mention in *The Independent* • Representative may vote and run for board of directors

Library Subscription
Year's subscription to *The Independent* only

JOIN AIVF TODAY!

Membership Rates

- ❏ $25/student (enclose copy of student ID)
- ❏ $45/individual
- ❏ $75/supporting
- ❏ $75/library subscription
- ❏ $100/non-profit organization
- ❏ $150/business & industry
- ❏ Magazines are mailed Second-class; add $20 for First class mailing

Foreign Mailing Rates

- ❏ *Surface mail*
  (incl. Canada & Mexico) - Add $10
- ❏ *Air mail*
  —Canada, Mexico, Western Hemisphere- Add $20
  —Europe - Add $40
  —Asia, Pacific Rim, Africa - Add $50

Name(s) _____

Organization _____

Address _____

City _____

State _____ ZIP _____

Country _____

Weekday tel. _____

Fax _____

$_____ Membership cost

$_____ Mailing costs (if applicable)

$_____ Contribution to FIVF
(make separate tax-deductible check payable to FIVF)

$_____ Total amount enclosed (check or money order)

Or please bill my ❏ Visa ❏ MC

Acct # _____

Exp. date ❏❏

Signature _____

AIVF, 304 Hudson Street, 6th Floor, New York, NY 10013
(212) 807-1400 tel / (212) 463-8519 fax